HIV, AIDS, and the LAW

A Guide to Our Rights and Challenges

Mark S. Senak, J. D.

Director of Planning
AIDS Project Los Angeles (APLA)
Los Angeles, California

Foreword by
Tim Sweeney

Former Executive Director
Lambda Legal Defense Fund
and Former Executive Director
Gay Men's Health Crisis

 **INSIGHT BOOKS**

Plenum Press • New York and London

KF3803.A54 S46 1996
Senak, Mark S.
HIV, AIDS, and the law : a
guide to our rights and   n-Publication Data
challenges

Senak, Mark S.
    HIV, AIDS, and the law : a guide to our rights and challenges
  Mark S. Senak ; foreword by Tim Sweeney.
      p.   cm.
    Includes bibliographical references and index.
    ISBN 0-306-45268-5 (hardbound). -- ISBN 0-306-45269-3 (pbk.)
    1. AIDS (Disease)--Patients--Legal status, laws, etc.--United
States. 2. Gay men--Legal status, laws, etc.--United States.
I. Title.
KF3803.A54S46   1996
344.73'04369792--dc20
[347.3044369792]   96-4185
                                                             CIP

It is extremely important to know that the information presented in this book, except where otherwise specifically noted, speaks to general legal principles that have developed around HIV, and not to what the specific law may be in your city, county, or state. This is meant to be a guide, not a road map. Its purpose is to give you history and background so that when you seek legal help, whether you are a person with HIV, someone who works with HIV, or a health care professional, you understand the issues well enough to be a more potent force in your own protection.

ISBN 0-306-45268-5 (Hardbound)
ISBN 0-306-45269-3 (Paperback)

© 1996 Mark S. Senak
Insight Books is a Division of Plenum Publishing Corporation
233 Spring Street, New York, N.Y. 10013-1578

An Insight Book

10 9 8 7 6 5 4 3 2 1

Printed in the United States of America

HIV, AIDS, and the LAW

A Guide to Our Rights and Challenges

This book is dedicated to my sister,
Paula Hubbard, who made me read my first book,
and to my mother, Kathleen Senak,
who kept faith that I could write my first one,
and in loving memory of my partner, Joseph Foulon.

FOREWORD

GRID, HTLV, AIDS, HIV, PWA .... There are many acronymns that come with acquired immune deficiency syndrome. Understanding this disease requires a person to make a conscious effort to learn a new vocabulary. The frustration of patients, care partners, and advocates is heightened by the scientific, medical, and bureaucratic lingo that is central to confronting how we live with this disease. It has been in that initial contact with the disease that I have seen so many people challenge what they are told and assert a right to meet this disease on their own terms.

HIV, AIDS, and the Law: A Guide to Our Rights and Challenges is a self-help guide for those individuals and families affected by HIV who want to define the disease on their own terms. It has the legal terms and advice that will give practical guidance to people; it has the real life stories of people with HIV to give context, support, and hope that challenging this disease is a way of life and it is worth living every day to its fullest.

I first heard of AIDS when the *New York Times* ran an article in July 1981 under the headline "Rare Cancer Seen in 41 Homosexuals." At that time, I was the executive director of Lambda Legal Defense and Education Fund, a lesbian and gay civil rights organization that engages in test case litigation to further the human rights of gay people. I was twenty-six years old and fortunately had had little personal experience with the medical or health care system. Within months, I would be thrown into a world of cancers, pneumonia, viruses, and public health laws ranging from partner notification to quarantine. I would be discussing blood banks, privacy of medical records, disability eligibility, hemophilia, and contamination of syringes. While trying to absorb all these new

vii

issues, I began to experience, along with many in the lesbian and gay community, a wrenching fear and foreboding about our future. Elements of society that had been looking for an excuse for their homophobia found their answer in AIDS. The 70% of the American public that consistently believed that homosexuality was immoral and unnatural had their deepest suspicions confirmed.

During that same period, a group of very brave men and women defied convention and decided that despite the catastrophic predictions, they were going to change the course of this epidemic by trying to save as many lives as possible. Against overwhelming fear, stigma, and violence, individuals overcame their own doubts and ignorance and set the world on the path to a cure and vaccine. The persons with AIDS (PWA) movement challenged, changed, and inspired us all.

I remember discussions with colleagues at Lambda, Gay Men's Health Crisis, American Civil Liberties Union, National Gay and Lesbian Task Force, the People with AIDS Coalition, AIDS Action Council, and American Foundation for AIDS Research, where we sketched out the possible negative ramifications of the emerging disease and went to work on political and legal strategies to demand a new approach to this public health crisis. Given the fear and loathing associated with sexuality and injection drug use, coupled with the rising tides of intolerance and anti-immigrant feeling, we knew we must be creative and think of solutions that effectively married both good public health practice and preservation of basic civil rights. We had to master the legal and political systems to develop or expand concepts such as anonymous HIV-antibody testing centers, voluntary partner notification and counseling, health-care proxies, and antidiscrimination laws as they applied to disabling illnesses. We had to make the political and legal systems understand AIDS from the point of view of gay men, injection drug users, people of color, women, and the uninsured.

When I went to work at Gay Men's Health Crisis as deputy director in 1986, I saw the practical application of these policy and legal strategies. Mark Senak was already at GMHC as the director of legal services. I saw how legal and financial clinics gave information and direction to individuals and families impacted by HIV. I saw how one person could take on a hospital, home care company, or—better yet—a private insurance company or city human resources agency and demand respect and services. A basic tenet of the AIDS movement, "information is power," was proving as powerful and effective as any medicine.

I also witnessed the importance of being an "informed consumer" when my older brother Mark came down with AIDS. Using the GMHC legal and financial advocacy services, he refused to give in to the overwhelming technical terms and demanded and received services that helped him live a longer and fuller life—a life with many more concrete resources and on terms of his own design.

Mark Senak has written a helpful and hopeful book that is based on his fourteen years of work on the front lines of the epidemic. It reflects the author's belief that life can and must be fully lived on one's own terms. We owe him a debt of gratitude for showing us a way to face this epidemic one day at a time.

Tim Sweeney
Former Executive Director,
Lambda Legal Defense Fund, and
Former Executive Director,
Gay Men's Health Crisis

PREFACE

A Brief and Personal History of AIDS and the Law

AIDS does not make victims. People do. People do it to others,
they do it to themselves. History has shown us that people have
been motivated to go to extraordinary lengths to grab and hold on
to their personal rights and freedoms. Documents such as the
Magna Carta and the *Declaration of Independence* are drawn up
declaring rights for common people. Great works in literature are
written by dissidents such as Alexander Solzhenitsyn. Revolutions
establish a whole new order and institutionalize the dignity of each
person with a guarantee of rights. These are examples of what
happens when people get together and decide to take authority and
control over their own destinies rather than be victimized by
circumstances or the opinions of others.

History is also a testament to situations where people have
been powerless or unwilling to exert power. There have been
periods when tyranny, for a time, would rule, until a movement
among people brought about circumstances that caused oppression to stop—the most dramatic example in modern history perhaps being the collapse of the Iron Curtain. But the pursuit of rights
on any scale, for individuals or for an entire nation, involves
immense challenges. There are, at times, seemingly impossible
obstacles to be overcome. Rights do not usually flow as a matter of
nature; they are pursued and won and defended. It is as true for
each nation as it is for each person.

In 1982, the rights of people with AIDS were virtually nonexistent, as there were no laws regarding disease-specific classes of
people. Protections for people rested in the context of disability
laws, and in those early years AIDS was not yet recognized as a

disability by legal standards. There was no AIDS-specific legislation because AIDS did not exist prior to 1982. Yet by 1994 there were hundreds of laws concerning AIDS. Because people cared to make a change, rights for people with HIV/AIDS were won. The challenge today is to negotiate those laws and one's circumstances so that one's rights are protected, defended, and maintained.

When I first began work with people with AIDS as a volunteer, it was with an organization formed in the early 1980s called the Bar Association for Human Rights of Greater New York (BAHR-GNY). One snowy evening in early 1983, I went to the home of a lawyer where a meeting was being held not long after the epidemic began. A group of attorneys had begun doing *pro bono* work in answer to the dire legal needs being experienced by people with a new disease that, as yet, did not really have a name or a known cause. There weren't many lawyers, just enough to fit into a small living room in Manhattan's Upper West Side. But they were a group of legal pioneers who were willing to go into hospital rooms at a time when nurses and doctors were still often afraid to do so, and they did it for the purpose of helping the patient write a last will and testament. Like most pioneering people, this group, led by Professor Art Leonard of New York Law School and Stephen Gittleson, a private practice attorney, were brave without even knowing it. They were people dedicated to doing what needed to be done for the benefit of people with AIDS, and others soon followed.

At that time, I had not yet knowingly met a person with the disease nor, since I was in the corporate practice of law, had I ever done a will. Yet in 1983, wills were the most pressing need of persons with AIDS (PWAs), who were dying so quickly. Later, PWAs would need help with insurance, discrimination, and landlord/tenant, debtor/creditor, and other related issues simply because of their AIDS diagnoses.

At the time, I was working with a firm that invested foreign funds in U.S. real estate projects. My closest experience with mortality was my father's death while I was in law school. He suffered an agonizing death from cancer that reduced him to a skeleton within only a few months of diagnosis. Seeing that happen to him frightened me. I could not have realized that my experience with him was a mere foreshadowing of the next several years with friends and clients. My wills expertise was limited to a good grade in my class on the subject in law school, but I never actually had to write one.

This basis of knowledge of both wills and mortality was not a very big one from which to make a leap. In the coming years I would learn a lot about both, and I would learn it fast. Wills class in a law school lecture room crowded with eager future lawyers of America did little to prepare me for what it would be like to sit across from people younger than myself and ask them how they would like to dispose of their bodily remains. Nor did it prepare me for countless deathbed scenes during which, at the age of 30, like my *pro bono* panel colleagues, I would have to guide the hand of people younger than myself to assist them in affixing their signature on their last will and testament. I learned quickly that law school is all theory.

The first client who was assigned to me was a vice president of a large publishing company. He was coming to my house on a Saturday afternoon for our initial interview. I was quite nervous and spent the morning straightening and then restraightening my apartment before his arrival. I was terribly afraid of him. He represented everything of which I was most afraid. I really didn't want him in my apartment. I really didn't want to face him, his illness, or his eventual death. He represented everything I wanted to avoid. Faced with no choice, however, I overcame my fear. Countless times since then, I have seen many individuals, landlords, employers, friends, and families of PWAs often have the same fears. Sometimes they are able to overcome them; when they cannot, the PWA usually suffers some form of discrimination or loss of benefits.

AIDS has challenged our society on a number of levels as no other phenomenon has in this century since the Great Depression. We are all afraid. We would all like to avoid the things AIDS represents to us. However, society has a responsibility to act rationally in the face of that fear or we stand to lose lives.

Admittedly, I did not understand this great scheme of things on that Saturday. I only knew I was doing something that I thought was the right thing to do. When the client came to my apartment, I was more ill at ease than he was. Even though it was his mortality we were discussing, it was *my* mortality that I began to contemplate. I offered him something to drink and he asked for water. After he left, I sterilized the glass in boiling water for 10 minutes.

It has been a long journey for me since that time. It has been a long journey for us all. Hundreds of thousands have died and, in the course of the tragedy that has been AIDS, painful lessons have been learned. It is my hope that, in reading some of what has developed in the legal arena for people living with AIDS, further pain can be avoided and that individuals who are suffering from the oppression offered by disease and its effects can be empowered to end that oppression in their lives.

ACKNOWLEDGMENTS

This book was a daunting task for me. I am happy to say it was not a lonely one. I want to thank first of all Randye Retkin, Mark Scherzer, David Schulman, and Liz Cooper not only for their expertise but also for their dedication to the notion of what is right and for the loyalty and strength they have lent people with HIV. I need also to say that working with kind editors, whose unique combination of patience and vision made this book possible, was a wonderful experience. Special thanks are due to Frank Darmstadt and Jennifer Reynolds.

I need also to acknowledge the patience, support, kindness, encouragement, and offers to help of my worthy assistant, Flint Ternes, who helped me get through every day a little more organized than I was the day before and who made work a fun experience for me. I need to thank my agent Jed Mattes just for being Jed Mattes. I would like also to thank Raymond Davidson for his mentoring and support. In addition, this task would have been immeasurably more difficult without the encouragement I received from Michael Lombardo, Kate Graber, Susan Connelly, Steven Bing, Dan Bross and Bob Cundall, Tim Sweeney, Jim Bozora and Jon Mills, Mike Prelip, and Dia Anthony and Bruce Anderson. And for their technical support and provision of resources, I must thank Jacques Chambers, Craig Koendarfer, Tom Barnes, and Rosemarie Benitez. My boss and friend, Jimmy Loyce, Jr., gave me words of encouragement, lunch, and allowed me to take vacation days when I needed them—all were essential. Thanks too to my cat, Ginger Pye, and dogs, Ricky and Lucy, who put up with late dinners and short walks without complaint and with steadfast loyalty.

And as for my friend Mark Hemphill, who in 1983 took me to my first meeting of lawyers who were getting together to do *pro bono* work for people with AIDS, I have not yet decided whether to thank him or to sue him.

CONTENTS

INTRODUCTION

Between the covers of this book, you will see portrayed some of the greatest legal challenges that face an individual with HIV. You will also see how, as a consequence of the epidemic, gay men and lesbians can obtain more rights than existed before the epidemic—rights that will make the law respect nontraditional relationships, win entitlements, secure property, and protect employment and access to health care. They are not rights that will flow naturally, they are rights for which one must often take up a fight and aggressively assert oneself. Therein lie the challenges for affected individuals.

While guiding the reader through some of the most basic issues faced by an individual, this book also provides a historical perspective on how those issues developed over time. Starting with the first chapter on wills and powers of attorney, the reader will quickly see how the issues that at first impacted only the individual began to spill over and affect an ill-prepared society as a whole. Therein lie the challenges for society.

In 1983, the Gay Men's Health Crisis took on a legal services program to serve people with AIDS in their growing need, staffing it with volunteers from the Bar Association for Human Rights of Greater New York (BAHR-GNY). Although the program's initial purpose was to do wills and powers of attorney, it quickly became more when PWAs began to have more diverse needs. When a lawyer interviewed one of these clients for a will, the experience would seem less like a will session and more like a bar exam question, where you have to spot the issues as they arise in a complicated narrative. During a will interview, a person with AIDS would reveal so many causes of action involving so many areas of the law that it was hard for a lawyer to know where to begin.

For instance, while telling a lawyer about his estate, a client might question the necessity for even making a will since he had so little money left anyway now that he had lost his insurance, was fired from his job, and had incurred moving expenses after his landlord or his roommate or his lover had kicked him out. For some if not most people with AIDS, financial and social support networks erode faster than their immune systems, with effects that can be almost as deadly. In response, the BAHR-GNY *pro bono* panel set up a safety net of free legal services that attempted to meet some of the most basic legal needs of people with AIDS. New York was the first place in the United States where AIDS impacted women and children began being orphaned by the scourge of AIDS. As a result, custody issues needed to be addressed. Once medical treatments improved and people began living longer, they needed more in the way of legal services. AIDS needed to be recognized as a disability for purposes of getting support from traditional disability programs. People with AIDS living on limited and fixed incomes had to deal with the burden of debt they acquired before their disability, or with the advent of high medical costs and non-covered prescriptions after their disability. And discrimination was a rampant and natural reaction to AIDS; social security personnel often refused to handle the application of a person with AIDS because they were afraid of contagion.

Rock Hudson's announcement in 1985 that he had developed AIDS brought AIDS from the background of the consciousness of the nation to the foreground with no accompanying education. In fact, if you were to ask, many people would identify 1985 as the year AIDS began, because that is the first year that the media made America aware of it. However, a little knowledge became a terrible thing. Without accompanying AIDS education, the general response was panic, and discrimination became widespread. People lost their jobs, their access to public accommodations, and their homes.

The legal system reacted strongly to acts of discrimination. Existing statutes against discrimination were enforced and new legislation specifically protecting people with HIV was enacted. These events, occurring first on a local level, culminated in the passage of the Americans with Disabilities Act by Congress in 1990.

While discrimination was outlawed on the job, in housing, and in public accommodation, it remained legal for the insurance industry. People with HIV were dropped by their insurers and those who had bought individual policies of insurance found that they were charged with material misrepresentation by insurers that refused to cover preexisting conditions. People found that their neighborhoods had been redlined by insurance companies. Companies engaged in businesses suspected by insurers of employing a high concentration of homosexuals found that they could not purchase group insurance. Even AIDS service organizations, such as AIDS Project Los Angeles (APLA), were dropped from insurance rosters and had trouble finding coverage for their employees. Increasingly, insurance companies shirked their responsibilities by refusing to cover people with HIV and their conditions, sending them to the ranks of those who relied on the already-burdened public health delivery system. In short, insurers systematically shifted the burden of this epidemic to the taxpayer.

Thus legal issues facing individuals began to have direct impact on society's institutions, particularly health-care providers. The talk show circuit buzzed with debates over the rights of the infected versus the rights of the uninfected. Testing in various settings took on a momentum the consequences of which were not always foreseeable. People tended to view the new HIV antibody test as a medical tool, but in fact the test became one of not only health or illness, but legality, insurability, employability, and even friendship and family. The test became a marker for discrimination and fear.

Use of the HIV test in the medical setting was first viewed by some as a measure to "protect" the health-care worker. But with the dramatic diagnosis of Kimberly Bergalis, along with five others allegedly infected by a dentist, the tables turned. Suddenly there was a demand for testing the health-care workers themselves. The climate of fear and discrimination reached new heights, no longer affecting only people with HIV or those suspected of HIV. No longer the scourge of the individual, whole systems became "AIDS victims."

Consequently, in support of a public health approach that relied on people to come forward voluntarily to be tested for HIV, legislation was enacted that would bolster the antidiscrimination supports already in place and would guarantee the confidentiality of those who tested.

The response of the legal system to the virus has been tremendously thoughtful and energetic. The epidemic has not only forced society to evaluate the delivery of health care in this country, but also impacted our legal and ethical systems to a degree second only to that experienced by medicine and science. Not since the Great Depression of 1929, when the breakdown of the nation's financial system inspired states to pass blue-sky security laws and the federal government to create the Securities and Exchange Commission, has the legal system been so responsive to an extraordinary event.

On the following pages those events unfold, not only as they affected individual people but also as they then affected everyone. Perhaps most interestingly, besides documenting the plight of individuals, the story of these events shows how the public's fear of mortality and of AIDS resulted in taboos and other irrational behaviors on a societal level. That behavior continues today as reflected in such public policy proposals as mandatory testing and the reporting of names. Each year, between 300 and 500 bills having to do with some aspect of AIDS and HIV infection are introduced before the various state legislatures of the nation. Antidiscrimination legislation is passed by the same legislatures that must then process proposals for mandatory testing in a range of venues from prisons to marriage chapels to hospitals. The formation of public policy around AIDS is not always based on reason. Restrictive laws about education, insurance, and access to health care, as well as the revival of arcane laws that have little meaning in the face of the epidemic, clearly express societal fear and denial. For instance, in Utah two women sued to overturn a law, passed in 1987, that nullifies the marriage of any person carrying HIV. (They were successful and the law has been overturned.) Stephen J. Reese, the state senator who sponsored the bill, commented in 1993, "I don't even know what we were thinking." The pages that follow describe other experiences of individuals with AIDS and the obstacles faced by their advocates in the epidemic's first decade.

People who live with HIV infection or AIDS have repeatedly stated a preference not to be called "AIDS victims." The stigma of that term implies a state of helplessness, a passive waiting for something to happen. The preferred description is "person living with AIDS" or "person with AIDS," so that the active struggle to live is dignified as something other than helplessness. It was in recognition of this need that our group of lawyers got together during the early days of the epidemic in New York. We realized that a person becomes a victim not by virtue of a disease but by the failure of the system. We were determined to create a system that would permit as few victims as possible. We set up free legal services that grew into an enormous program helping thousands of people. We discovered that the law is more than a living, but an instrument of power and of empowerment.

1

Where There Is a Will, There Is a Way

All men think all men mortal but themselves.

Edward Young (1683–1765)
Night Thoughts, Night I, line 424

Writing a will is a manifestation of mortality and is morbid—difficult for most people to think about and even more difficult to do. The idea of calling a lawyer and saying that you want to write a will may not even occur to you until you are old, sick, or have acquired an amount of property that you could seriously refer to as an "estate" worth giving away. Excuses to put writing off a will are within the scope of even the most limited imagination. In other words, talk is cheap.

"I'm not old enough to write a will."

"I can write it myself."

"I'm not sick and don't need a will."

"I don't have enough property to write a will."

But the fact is that writing a will is not just about owning property, and it is not just about dying. It is not something you should do because you are sick and it is not morbid. In fact, for people with HIV/AIDS in particular, writing a will can be important not because they are in a life-threatening situation but because it affords an unexpected opportunity to get back some of the authority and control over life that is sometimes lost with an HIV diagnosis. Writing a will is much less about property than it is about making decisions about events or about what will happen to particular people, places, and possessions.

7

So it is best to think of it in these terms—you are writing a will because it is your free and unrestrained exercise of power over what is going to occur even when you are no longer here to do anything about it. Just think of it as a "power trip."

BACKGROUND

For the most part, people who face an illness like HIV disease, experience a genuine and anguished lack of power, authority, and control over their lives as a direct consequence of being sick. In one form or another, they are betrayed by what occurs inside the body, something that is beyond not only their own control but also that of modern science and medicine. Bodily aches and pains are sudden in their appearance and begin to limit physical movement. Kaposi's Sarcoma, a skin cancer, may suddenly form lesions, first on an arm or ankle, then on an ear or the nose. One day they feel fine, then, with little warning, comes the shortness of breath, a fever, a trip to the hospital, and a diagnosis of pneumocystis caranii pneumonia. Or, with a disease known as Progressive Multifocal Leukoencephalopathy (PML), a person with AIDS may lose control over bodily functions, much like a person with Lou Gehrig's disease though at a much more accelerated rate. In short, persons with AIDS (PWAs) may be losing control over their bodies. At the same time, other people respond to them differently than before they were sick. That too is beyond their control and authority.

In the case of a person diagnosed with HIV or AIDS, these perceptions may be exaggerated by a medical and public lack of awareness of the disease as well as by the stigma attached to the syndrome and the people most affected by it. (See Chapters 5 and 8 for discussions of stigma.) These attitudes also seem beyond control. Like many other catastrophic illnesses, AIDS is more than a syndrome brought on by disease; it is a metaphor for an utter lack of control over our bodies and our environment.

For gays, lesbians, and minorities, as disenfranchised people, lack of control has always been an issue because as individuals they have never been able to control mainstream society's biases against them. Now, compounded by HIV, control over prejudice is even more out of their grasp. In addition to the stigma they suffered because of *who* they were—gay, African American, Hispanic—they stand to lose family, friends, jobs, and economic security because of *what* they are —people with AIDS.

While the act of preparing a will may not be the most obvious route to restoring control and authority to a person's life, it can in fact be a very empowering experience. To write a will is to take the law by its collar, pull it down to eye level, and say, "You are going to respect me, my wishes, and my relationships with people who are important to *me*—and you are going to do it *my* way." For instance, a will may be the very way, in fact the only way, for a same-sex couple to enjoy most of the rights of a married couple, for the first time forcing the law to respect their relationship. To understand how, it is necessary to understand what a will is all about.

A WILL DEFINED—PROPERTY AND RIGHTS

A will is an instrument that you draw up, usually with the help of a lawyer, to outline your wishes for the dispensation of rights you possessed while alive. In your will, you bestow these rights on people who are important to you. They can be family members or they can be people who are not related to you but whom you regard as family or as deserving. The will allows you to have a say when you are no longer here to exercise those rights.Because of this, *a will is only valid after its subject is deceased*. Thus, a will is different from a power of attorney, which is only valid while its subject is alive.

We tend to think of property as something that we own outright, but what we actually own are rights over the property. A will should not be viewed as an instrument for giving away property ownership but for granting rights over certain properties that you own. If you have paid for your property entirely, you own almost all the rights over it. If you have only paid for part of it, you own some rights over it while others are held by the creditor who loaned you the money for the purchase. Each day each of us exercises rights over our property. Property, if you will, is merely a physical manifestation of power, a tangible representation of a person's rights.

From this perspective, a will becomes less morbid, more an exercise of power. View it less as "I'm giving away my property because I am dying" than as "I am going to design a distribution of power and it will be absolute power."

The reason it is important to dilute the "property" concept of a will is that often PWAs or those with other chronic illnesses are left with little money or property. Frequently, the ravages of AIDS are not confined to the physical but extend to the financial as well. For the ill, the thought of making a will may seem moot. Nothing could be further from the truth.

In the epidemic's early days, medical treatment for HIV/AIDS was very different. People with AIDS died quickly; a diagnosis generally meant that the person was dead within a few months.[*] Dr. Scott Hitt, a gay Los Angeles physician and the chairperson of the Presidential Advisory Council on HIV/AIDS, characterizes the change this way: "When I talk to patients, I tell them the difference between 1987 and today," he says. "Even in 1988, if someone came into my office and told me they were a new patient and stated they had pneumocystis pneumonia [PCP] six months earlier, I would regard them as a long term survivor." Now, however, the treatment scene is very different: "Now it is quite common for people who come into my office to have had pneumonia three years before. We know instinctively that people are living longer." Dr. Hitt also cites the fact that treatment for opportunistic infections has also improved dramatically: "We used to have only one preventive treatment for PCP; now we have many, along with preventions for several other opportunistic infections."

---

*People with HIV can live many years and, in fact, there are theories that some people with HIV may never develop AIDS. Yet many in the general public still believe that an HIV diagnosis is equivalent to an AIDS diagnosis and that death will occur within a few months or years.

In addition to improvements in treatment, public education has improved. Early in the epidemic, people did not know that they were HIV positive or even that they were infected with the virus. There was no name for the virus and because the virus had not yet been discovered, there was no test. People were reluctant to enter the hospital room of someone with this new disease. People found out they had AIDS when one day, like a lightning bolt, they developed a shortness of breath that subsequently was diagnosed as PCP or a spot on the skin that meant Kaposi's Sarcoma.

An average person has between 800 and 1200 T cells, which help the body to fight off infection. Early in the epidemic, before tests, people discovered they had AIDS only when they became sick, when the immune system was already compromised. With very few T cells left, usually below 200; there was little time for intervention, medical or otherwise. People barely had time to make a will before a host of opportunistic infections defeated them. Today, in contrast, an HIV test might reveal that one is HIV-positive while the immune system is still functioning well, with a normal number of T cells. It may be many years before an opportunistic infection develops.

In many early cases, the will was written at the deathbed. This was a difficult setting for the exercise of control. Physically, the exercise was challenging. Before much was known about AIDS, hospitals required persons going into a patient's room to "suit up," donning mask, gloves, and gown. People involved in the will signing were distracted by the dramatic circumstances of life support and the suffering of the patient. Medical tests were being conducted by hospital personnel. Moreover, lucidity of the person doing the will could be called into question later. Today, Dr. Hitt advises that this situation be avoided where possible. "In the last few weeks before dying, a majority of patients do experience some confusion. If there is any question of their not being of sound mind, then there is an increased likelihood of a challenge to the will."

In addition, family and significant others were sometimes present, often in contention with one another. Especially in the early days, a family often received the news of their son's AIDS diagnosis simultaneously with the news that their son was gay. Dr. Hitt asserts that this is still very true today: "There are many instances where families find out that their son is gay and that he has AIDS at the same time. Usually a couple of family members, a cousin, or a close sibling may be aware, but the rest of the family has been left in the dark."

Motivations—Why People Make Wills

Property is not the sole guiding factor in writing a will; there are others that often are psychosocial in nature. Lawyers don't usually warm up to words like "psychosocial;" and most probably couldn't define them. "Psychosocial" evokes "feelings" and is far removed from solid legal terminology. Social workers talk about feelings quite a bit, using words like "sharing"; meanwhile, most people think that the closest expression in the legal vocabulary to the concept of sharing is the term "contingency fee." Nevertheless, it is essential for a lawyer to have a good grasp of the psychosocial ramifications of life-threatening illnesses. If you are a consumer looking for a lawyer, and you interview a lawyer who doesn't seem to grasp this truth, keep looking.

While in the early days of the epidemic people often made their wills at the last minute because they hadn't known they were sick, such delays today are often more a function of strong denial about the serious life-threatening nature of the situation. Breaking through denial is not easy. In fact, denial may be perfectly healthy. Dr. Hitt notes that soon after diagnosis with HIV "there is a lot of denial. Once, however, there is an opportunistic infection, denial erodes. People will deny the possibility of getting ill until they do. But," he adds, "denial can be a perfectly appropriate response to some situations." Though a person may be defeated by rigid denial, denial does exist for good reasons.

For example, a state of denial may buy a person enough time to keep him from panicking. Like a little voice inside, denial argues that this emergency really isn't an emergency after all: "I don't have to be scared. I'll just pretend it isn't happening." Later, once he can see his way out of the emergency, denial may no longer be necessary. Thus, a skillful lawyer is also a social worker, understanding the psychosocial ramifications of the client's situation. Denial can be strong, but it can be necessary. It can also become dysfunctional. Dr. Hitt encounters someone who waits until it is too late "every month at least." Nevertheless, whether useful or dysfunctional, denial should not be taken away unless it is replaced by something else.

That "something else" can be one of several mechanisms. For example, using a will to recover some of the power, authority, and control that has been lost as a consequence of AIDS can help overcome denial. One volunteer attorney related the following story:

> David, a Broadway actor, contacted a lawyer to do a will for him. When it came time for the initial interview, however, David was experiencing a great deal of trouble concentrating on what he wanted to do.The lawyer was unsure whether David didn't actually know what he wanted to do, or whether, like a great many people facing a life-threatening situation, David was in denial about his situation and avoiding doing the will. The lawyer knew that clients who have will appointments frequently call to cancel because they are "feeling better."
>
> David had, in fact, canceled several appointments. Sometimes he kept the appointment, but when the lawyer arrived, he did not really want to discuss the specifics of his will, only the legal generalities so that he could understand it better.
>
> Then, David was dying. He had systemic tuberculosis, and his weight fell to only 100 pounds. David made a third appointment to attempt once more to get down onto paper what it was that he wanted to do. But after an hour David still wouldn't talk. The lawyer noticed that on the wall of his bedroom hung several photographs of David performing on Broadway in various roles. The lawyer finally said in exasperation, "Look, David, this is your only chance to write, star in, produce, and direct your own production."
>
> David was quiet for a moment and looked at the photographs. Then he started to dictate his last will and testament. He began by making bequests (gifts) of his juicer and then his vacuum cleaner. He had 32 separate bequests he wanted to make. It took three hours. The lawyer called it "Gone with the Will." But it was worth the time and effort because David finally made his will, and he caused the rights he had in his property to be given in a manner that otherwise would not

have occurred. He did not have much property to give but what he had was important to him.

David died shortly thereafter. For him, it had been necessary to put off the will because it was so much a manifestation of his mortality. For him, doing the will was an acceptance of his death. But when David saw that the opportunity to do the will was one in which he could exercise control and authority—"to write, star in, produce, and direct" his own production—he began to draw up "Gone with the Will."

As stated earlier, a will can demonstrate that a person is taking authority and control over *something* in the face of a situation where he or she is seemingly losing authority over *everything*.

For lesbian and gay couples, the incentive can be even more than the notion of exercising control. In writing a will, a lesbian or gay couple can, in many respects, get the marriage certificate that had always been denied. That sense of empowerment may be a force powerful enough to dislodge any denial.

When a heterosexual couple marches down an aisle before witnesses and takes an oath, saying the words "I do" before a person invested with power by the state, they are legally married. When you take away the guests, the music, the food, the ceremony, a marriage is essentially a legal contract between two people who are not of the same sex. They agree to live together and share certain assets, and the contract is recognized and enforced by the state in which the couple lives.

In fact, even when a heterosexual couple avoids a formal marriage ceremony, the two people may nevertheless find themselves married. In some states, the law will do it for them merely by virtue of the fact that the couple has cohabited for a set period of years, varying by state. This is called common-law marriage. Some states, such as New York, only recognize common-law marriages that occurred during a particular period of years when common law was recognized by the state.

Gay and lesbian couples enjoy no such recognition. Even with the recent passage of domestic partner laws in some jurisdictions, the right to inherit automatically from one's partner is nonexistent. Domestic partner laws usually affect only worker benefits, such as insurance coverage; they do not provide the full respect of the law for the couple. In no state, moreover, can a same-sex couple cohabit and be deemed married, no matter the years of cohabitation, any ceremony the partners have undergone, or the depth of their commitment and fidelity.

The law has a great deal of respect for the first relationship and none for the latter. For people who are married, either by ceremony or by common law, the law implicitly writes their contract, defining rights and even, by implication, spelling out how a divorce would proceed if ever needed. In addition, the law also automatically writes out their wills by delivering the estate to the spouse by virtue of the laws of intestacy.

When the Law Writes Your Will

Having written a valid will, you are "testate." To die without a will is to die "intestate," in which case certain laws govern what happens to your rights and property. In essence, then everyone has a "will" whether or not it is written on paper. Automatically "written" by law on your death, it is based on your legal relationship to other people. When you write your own will, these intestacy laws are essentially rewritten by you and can include people with whom you do not necessarily have a "legal" or blood relationship.

There is a general pattern to the ways that the laws of intestacy run.

(1) If you have a spouse and children, the law will usually provide for them out of the estate with some sort of division among them. If there is a spouse or children only, then the estate will go to them.

(2) If there is no spouse and there are no children, then the law delivers the estate to a parent, or, if both are living, in equal shares to each.

(3) If no parents, no spouse, and no children exist, then the law will look for brothers and sisters;

(4) then for aunts and uncles,

(5) then for cousins, and

(6) finally for grandparents.

At this point, if the law can find no relatives, then the state where you live steps in, generously relieving you of the burden of your estate.

To make a will is to choose for oneself who will have rights over the estate. If you have a parent from whom you are estranged and one with whom you are close, they will both inherit equally if you have no spouse or children unless a will is written. Your will forestalls the "default" formula set up in the laws of intestacy.

Gay Couples—Saying "I Do"

By virtue of the laws of intestacy, it may not be necessary for a legally married couple to write a will (though it is still advisable). Even without a will, a married couple will have many rights vis-à-vis their relationship and each other. These rights extend beyond the right to inherit one another's estate.

> On the day of their marriage, Alice and Joe are strolling down a street in postnuptial bliss. There is a terrible accident; while crossing a street, Joe is run down by a bus. Because the driver was drunk at the time, he did not see Joe, who was crossing legally at a light. Alice is unharmed but greatly upset as they arrive at the hospital. Joe, badly hurt, is placed into the hospital's intensive care unit (ICU). The physicians consult with Alice on a regular basis about Joe's condition. Because of his injuries, Joe is not capable of making his own medical decisions. Alice can make medical decisions for Joe because she is his wife, even if only for a few hours. Eventually, the primary physician comes to Alice to explain that Joe needs a respirator. He asks Alice if they have ever talked this over. She replies that they have indeed discussed it and that Joe had indicated to her on numerous occasions that he would *never* under *any* circumstances imaginable want to be placed on a respirator. "But," the doctor says, "it could be two days, or it could be two months. It may help, but it may not." "No," Alice says. "He would not want to be on the respirator." The physician respects her wishes.
> Joe dies. Though he did not have time to make a will, Alice

nevertheless inherits his estate under the laws of intestacy. She also can become the administrator of the estate. Further, as Joe's wife, she has the right to sue the bus driver and the bus company for the loss of her husband and to collect a judgment against them.

Because the law held the relationship of Alice and Joe in such high regard, they were well taken care of. She was able to see Joe in the hospital, make medical decisions for him, decide on funeral arrangements, inherit his estate, and sue and win compensation for his loss.

Now consider the same case, but this time of Frank and Joe.

In the case of Frank and Joe there is no wedding ceremony. They have lived together for twenty years in the same apartment, leased in Joe's name. Joe is estranged from his family, who live hundreds of miles away, because they do not accept that he is a gay man. One day, while crossing the street, Joe is struck by a drunken bus driver. Seriously injured, he is taken to the hospital, where it is decided that he will be placed in ICU. The hospital has a firm policy that *only* family members may visit in ICU, so Frank is not permitted to see Joe. Frank is also excluded from all medical decision making. Joe's parents, to whom he hasn't spoken in years, arrive from out of town. When the proposal to put Joe on a respirator is presented by the physician, Joe's parents agree, because to do otherwise would be out of accord with their religious beliefs. Frank affirms that he and Joe discussed this possibility many times and that Joe stated repeatedly that he did not want to be put onto a respirator. Nevertheless, Joe spends several days on the respirator before he dies.

Because there is no will, Joe's parents stand to inherit the entire estate. Joe's family bars Frank from the apartment. They take all of Joe's things and many of Frank's as well. Because Joe is the leaseholder, in some states the law may presume that everything in the apartment is part of his estate. Joe's parents decide to have the body taken to their home for burial, in spite of the fact that Joe had told Frank he wanted to be cremated. Frank, with nothing left and few options, wants to sue the bus driver for his negligence but finds that he is without any legal "standing" to sue. Only family members have such standing, and if they sue, the estate would receive the money and they would inherit it. Frank is left alone with his grief, his memories, and the shirt on his back, but little else.

The difference between these two scenarios is vast, but it need not be. If Joe and Frank had made wills, they would have been protected against the kind of helplessness illustrated here. They too could have found themselves with all of the rights Alice and Joe held automatically. The will could, in effect, have served as a marriage certificate for Frank and Joe; they would have been proactive by taking some legal steps to have the law legitimize their relationship.

If Joe had made a will that left his possessions to his friend and companion, Frank, not Joe's parents, would have inherited the estate. Further, if Frank were named the executor of the estate, then he would have had standing to sue the bus driver and the bus company, because it is the duty of the executor to recover all sums owed to the estate. Then, when the recovery was awarded, as the sole beneficiary of the will he would have inherited the judgment as well. In effect, for many legal purposes Frank and Joe would have been married, or at least would have achieved many of the rights to inherit and sue that a married couple would have had under the same circumstances. To provide for consultations with the physician and the right to make medical and business decisions, they would have had to fill out some additional forms, called powers of attorney.

Powers of Attorney

A power of attorney is the delegation of authority to another individual to do that which you have the right to do yourself.

A power of attorney can be broad or specific, last forever or for a limited time, and be stated broadly, effective for all purposes, or stated only for *specific* purposes. The instrument can take effect immediately upon signing, or it can take effect only with the occurrence of a subsequent event, such as disability. There are different types of power of attorney for general, financial, and business use.

Joe is going on vacation for three months to Europe. He wants his friend Frank to pay his bills for him while he is gone. Joe trusts Frank to do so, but as a safeguard, he estimates the number of bills that will have to be paid. He has a financial power of attorney drawn up, which allows Frank to write checks from his account. In the power of attorney, Joe states that it shall only be valid from October 1 through December 31. Further, the power of attorney affects checks numbered 1000 through 1100 and only in amounts not to exceed $100.

This example concerns a financial power of attorney, but one can delegate almost any authority to another individual. Whether or not a power of attorney can be used for medical decisions depends on the state you live in. In the early days of the epidemic in New York, medical powers of attorney were written for people with HIV by volunteer attorneys who provided free legal services to people with AIDS. The power of attorney can be written very broadly or with a narrow focus, as long as its intent is clear. In the case of people with HIV, medical powers of attorney can be written to extend the right to another person to make medical decisions for the principle if the principle is no longer able to make those decisions himself or herself. Thousands of these were signed in the early days of the epidemic in New York.

Some lawyers believed that these documents were not legally valid in that some individual powers cannot be delegated to another because they are simply too personal. For example, you cannot delegate your right to vote to another person. Similarly, it was argued, one should not be able to delegate something so personal as medical decision making. There was no statute specifically stating that such a delegation could be made. In reality, however, hundreds of people were flooding the health-care system with new and ongoing cases of "full-blown AIDS." Physicians found themselves with a large population of extremely ill people who, generally speaking, did not have family in New York but who did have a friend or significant other willing to assist in the medical decision making. With the signed document in hand, the physician felt more comfortable talking to *someone* about the decisions to be made rather than acting in a vacuum with the presumed best interests of the patient in mind. "There is nothing more frustrating," says Dr. Hitt, "than when someone is gravely ill and alone, and you look in the chart and there is no one to talk to." But, he emphasizes, the problem goes beyond mere frustration. "These patients," he states, "can die in pain and go through things they may never have wanted to otherwise go through." Dr. Hitt recalls one patient who was diagnosed with a severe case of meningitis but had written no power of attorney. His parents were nowhere to be found. "That patient died on a respirator," he says, "and I'm pretty sure he wouldn't have wanted that, but without another person making that decision, I had to do it."

Still, the medical powers of attorney issued at the beginning of the epidemic did not have the official support of law. Thus, the New York State legislature in 1989 enacted legislation that statutorily guided the medical power of attorney. Likewise, California enacted legislation so strongly worded that a nonfamily member designated by a duly signed medical proxy statement now has preeminence over a nondesignated family member. Many other states also have specific legislation. If, in the earlier illustration, Joe had signed a medical power of attorney naming Frank, then Frank, not Joe's parents, would have made the decisions.

Taken together, the power of attorney document and a last will and testament form a powerful legal bond between two individuals. It is important to bear in mind the difference between the two documents, however. A will only concerns rights to be exercised after one's death and is only valid when, after one's death, it goes through a court procedure that declares it a valid instrument. A power of attorney, on the other hand, is a contract between the living and is only valid while the principle is alive. Once completed, these documents bestow rights and responsibilities on each party in a way that emulates Frank and Alice's situation, not the disastrous predicament of Frank and Joe. By writing wills, gay men and lesbians force the law to respect their relationships. Respect can be, and was, a powerful motivator for people at risk for HIV to overcome their denial, face the issues of mortality, and take control, gaining the validity and respect denied to them by the law for an entire lifetime. The most fundamental right, to marry the person you love, has always been denied. But where there is a will, there is a way.

WRITING AN ACTUAL WILL

You have seen what happens when the law writes your will for you. When you make your own, it is important to understand the mechanics of writing a will. One of the most frequent questions concerning the composition of a will is "Can't I just write it myself?" In fact, you can write it yourself in most states, and stationery shops frequently sell forms that you can fill in. However, just as it is not necessarily the best decision to let the law write it for you, it is also not always prudent to write it yourself. Remember, lawyers go to law school for a reason.

A will is only valid after one dies and after it is taken to court by the person who is named as the executor. The court examines it and, if all is in order, declares that it is valid, a process known as *probate*. The way the will is written and executed is the only means by which a court gets to know the testator, the person who made and signed the will.

Therefore, the court first scrutinizes the rights of those who would have inherited the estate had there been no will (under the laws of intestacy) and in doing so, looks with great care to the document itself to ensure that

- the will was not forged,
- there was no *undue influence* over the testator to write the will in a way different than would otherwise have occurred, and
- the testator was of sound mind when signing the will.

The court ensures that these conditions are fulfilled by assuring itself that the document has been drawn up and signed in accordance with the state's statutes. Therefore, the way a will is written or signed will determine whether or not it faces an easy time before the court during probate. If one of these conditions is not met, then the will might be challenged successfully, and, in fact, a violation of these conditions is the only way a will challenge can be success-ful. In looking at the will document and the circumstances sur-rounding its signing, the court looks for certain red flags warning that one of those three conditions may not, in fact, be satisfied and that the will demands further scrutiny. Lawyers, trained to know the law surrounding wills, can write them and have them signed in accordance with the statutes Since the objective of doing a will in the first place is to direct an orderly transfer of your rights over to people you choose, it makes sense to hire someone to do that who is trained to make that happen. In short, you definitely can write your own will, though different jurisdictions have different rules for doing it. Should you write your own will?

The Terms

Some terms are important in understanding who does what and how the will works, as well as to demystify some of the legal paraphernalia that is contained in the body of the document.

- *Administrator*: This is the person who, if there were no will (that is, if you died intestate), would oversee the estate in the same capacity as an executor (see below).
- *Article:* The will is made up of sections called articles. Each article may contain subparagraphs, particularly when it concerns various types of bequests. Different attorneys in different jurisdictions will differ in the way they draft the will. Nevertheless it is common to have the will divided in sections in this way. The articles are numbered.
- *Attorney draftsperson*: This is the attorney who is hired by the testator to write a will.
- *Beneficiary*: This is a person who is to receive the benefit of a gift. A will can name several, one, or even none. A beneficiary may also be the executor.
- *Bequest*: The will you are writing is designed to give rights that you have over people and property to other individuals. A bequest is best described as a gift of those rights. For

instance, the statement "I leave my interest in and to my home, located at 2020 Oak Drive" is a bequest.

- *Estate*: All that you own or are entitled to own is your estate. However, see below for differences in the kinds of estate possible.
- *Executor*: This is the person in charge of ensuring that your wishes stated in the will are carried out. After a person dies, the estate of the deceased is almost like an orphan child. An executor becomes its foster parent, with duties and responsibilities on behalf of that child. An executor is under a legal duty and obligation to pay all debts and expenses of the deceased from the estate (not from his or her own pocket), to get all monies due and owing to the estate, and to ensure the transfer as outlined in the bequests made under each article of the will. An executor may receive a fee for his duty, as prescribed by the law of the various states. An executor may also be a beneficiary in the will. An executor may be a nonfamily member.
- *In terrorem clause*: An *in terrorem* clause is sometimes put into a will to discourage will contests. It states that "I leave $10,000 to my friend, John Doe, but if John Doe should contest my will and lose that contest, he shall not inherit this bequest." It is a way of keeping people who might contest the will from doing so by, in effect, buying them off and giving them a negative incentive for doing so. This makes a will contest a win all or lose everything proposition.
- *Joint tenants*: Two people who jointly own property may have a right of survivorship connected with the ownership, so that if one predeceases the other, the survivor automatically inherits the property by operation of law and not under the terms of a will.
- *Legatee*: This is a person who would have inherited all or part of the estate had there been no will; in other words he would have received a legacy under the laws of intestacy.
- *Letters testamentary*: These are certificates issued by a court after it has examined a will and determined its validity.

These enable an executor to begin work on behalf of the estate.

- *Probate*: Probate is the process by which a court examines a will and determines that it is valid. If it deems it so, it issues letters testamentary to the executor of the will.
- *Residuary*: This is part of the estate. A will makes specific bequests, such as a car, a house, stocks, bonds, or cash. However, the articles of a will do not account for every type or kind of property. Therefore, after specific bequests are made, a residuary clause in the will takes care of the rest. It is the catch-all. The beneficiary of the residuary clause inherits all or part of the residuary estate and can be a person named in the will with a specific bequest or can be someone who hasn't been mentioned at all.
- *Tenants in common*: These are people who own property together but, unlike joint tenants, do not own it with a right of survivorship, and each interest is separate and apart from the other. In this case, a person's share of the property can be disposed of in the text of a will to a third party.
- *Testamentary estate*: This refers to that part of your property that you specify in the course of writing your will. Your testamentary estate is not everything you own, but a part of what you own.
- *Testamentary substitute*: Some property automatically passes to another person "by operation of law" upon one's death, without there having to be a will. For instance, a life insurance policy, an individual retirement account, real estate that you and another persons owned as joint tenants (but not as tenants in common), or joint checking or savings accounts, provide for transfer to the person who is named in a beneficiary statement or as joint owner automatically. These are not part of the testamentary estate and are not affected by the will. For example, if John Doe has a life insurance policy and has listed the beneficiary as Mary Doe, but in his will lists the beneficiary as Jane Doe, Mary Doe should still receive the funds, though it may enable Jane to make some

trouble. Such a slip could indicate that John Doe didn't know quite what he was doing when he made his will, potentially undermining his entire will.

- *Testator*: The person who is writing the will.
- *Will contest*: This is not a competitive event designed to see who wrote the best will. Nevertheless, a good will is important. A will contest occurs when a person with an interest challenges the validity of the will during the process of probate. Only three grounds are common in a will contest: (i) the testator did not sign the will; (ii) the testator was not of sound mind; and (iii) the testator was influenced by another against the testator's better judgment. These grounds for overturning a will are very difficult and very expensive to prove.
- *Witness*: A witness is a person who watches the testator sign the will and who then signs the will as well, attesting that the testator appeared of sound mind and body and signed of his or her own free will.

The Mechanics

The primary purpose of the will is to dispose of rights possessed by the testator to beneficiaries named by the testator. In doing so, one declines the provisions of the laws of intestacy in order to fulfill one's own wishes. In essence, the testator replaces the will the law writes automatically with his or her own.

By the laws of intestacy, the rights of the deceased are divided among legatees, those whom the laws of intestacy favor when a person dies without a will.

> Alice dies without a will. She is survived by only one sibling, Paul, and one cousin, Michael. She has a lover, Samantha. Under the laws of intestacy, Paul will inherit her entire estate. For this to happen, someone must become the administrator of her estate. The administrator can be anyone who petitions the court, but he or she will most likely need the permission of the legatees. In this case, there is only one legatee, Paul. Michael would only be a legatee if Paul were deceased. There-

fore, Paul is the most likely to step forward to be the administrator and would be obliged to pay all debts and expenses of
the deceased and of the estate out of proceeds from the estate.
Any assets left, he will transfer to himself. Samantha stands to
inherit nothing.

If Alice had decided to make a will, she would have decided who
inherits. She could have included Paul if she wanted to, but she
didn't have to. She could also have included Michael and
Samantha. She could have rejected all three in favor of another
person or a charity. She could have appointed anyone she
wanted as executor.

All this does not necessarily mean that one does a will for the
purpose of leaving family out.

Alice has both parents living and six siblings. Should she die
without a will, only her parents will inherit her estate, in equal
shares, as she has no spouse and no children. Her siblings
inherit nothing. Alice therefore writes a will leaving some
property to her parents and some to her siblings. Her lover,
Samantha, is a successful businesswoman, so she serves as the
executor of the estate.

How does everything get arranged? A model will form is provided
below with, next to it, my explanation for each article in italics. This
example is intended only to familiarize with the instrument itself;
it is not meant as a model to be used in drafting your own will.
Remember, each state has different rules.

MODEL LAST WILL AND TESTAMENT

I, John Smith, residing at 2020 Oak Drive, being of sound mind,
do hereby make this, my Last Will and Testament.

*The introductory paragraph declares that the testator is of sound mind
and that his address is his residence. The latter detail may seem trivial,
but when a person has more than one house, the introductory paragraph
indicates the one regarded as home. Additionally, in its small way, naming*

the address indicates that the testator was of sound enough mind to know where he lived.
FIRST: I hereby revoke all wills and codicils heretofore made by me.

The first article states that all prior wills and testaments are superseded by the current one. This statement is included regardless of whether the testator believes that he or she has ever made a will before.

SECOND: I hereby appoint my (good friend, mother, father, sister, brother, and so on) as Executor of my Last Will and Testament.

(OR)

I hereby appoint my (good friend[s], mother and father, friends and sister or brother, and so on) as Co-Executors of this, My Last Will and Testament.

(AND)

Should for any reason (_____) be unable or unwilling to serve as Executor, I hereby nominate my (good friend, mother, father, sister, brother, and so on) as Executor in (his/her/their) place and stead.

This article appoints an executor or co-executor. The person appointed should be trustworthy, with the mental and physical abilities to carry out the job, which can be arduous. Many times a person with AIDS will appoint a significant other who may also have AIDS. This choice is understandable, but consideration should be given to whether the significant other has the resources to accomplish the job. Often a significant other is devastated by the death of the testator, taking months before getting around to filing the will for probate. Appointing co-executors is an option, but the exercise of executorship will then depend on agreement among all parties, which may be difficult, considering the size of the job.

There is no legal reason why an executor cannot also be a beneficiary or the sole beneficiary and he or she does not have to be a family member.

It is recommended that an alternative executor be named. Should the executor be unable or unwilling to act, the executorship for the will is nevertheless provided for. This step also adds "shelf life" to the will by saving the testator the time, trouble, and expense of having to rewrite a will if it becomes apparent that the first executor will not be able to serve.

THIRD: I hereby give, devise, and bequeath the following property as follows:

(a) To my friend and companion, Joe Doe, I give, devise, and bequeath the sum of Ten Thousand Dollars ($10,000.00);

(b) To my mother and father, Jane and John Smith, I give, devise, and bequeath the sum of Five Thousand Dollars ($5,000), to be split evenly between the two of them, or if one should predecease me, then I give, devise, and bequeath the entire sum to their survivor;

(c) To the AIDS Project of Oaktown, I give, devise and bequeath the sum of One Thousand Dollars ($1,000).

These cash bequests are made absolutely out of the proceeds of the estate after payment of debts and expenses. If there is not enough cash in the estate, these bequests will not be made in their entirety, or if there is no money in the estate at all, the bequests will never be paid. It is important for the person making the will to demonstrate in the will that he or she knows and understands the limits of one's bounty, as it is evidence of testamentary capacity to know what the estate consists of. Grandiose or unrealistic gestures can threaten the will's validity. In this example, note that the testator's lover is referred to as "friend and companion" rather than "lover." While one may use whatever term one wants, it may be desirable to indicate a strong bond with terms that will not lead a homophobic judge to assume that the testator was guided not by reason but by lust in leaving substantial portions of the estate to a nonfamily member.

Note that the parents of the testator are left only $5,000. This bequest protects the will by showing that the testator did not "accidentally" overlook the parents. See In terrorem *clause in article sixth below.*

[OR]

THIRD: I hereby make the following cash gifts:

(a) To my friend and companion, Joe Doe, I give, devise, and bequeath the sum of Fifteen Thousand Dollars ($15,000);

(b) To the AIDS Project of Oaktown, I hereby give, devise, and bequeath the sum of One Thousand Dollars ($1,000);

(c) It is my stated intention herein to leave no cash bequest or bequest or gift of any other kind to my parents, John and Jane Doe.

The disinheriting of a relative need not be stated with rancor and emotion and, in fact, is probably better if not. A mere statement showing that the testator remembered that the relatives existed, followed by a clear, rational direction that no gift be provided to them is more reassuring to the probate court than an emotional statement that may raise the possibility of outside influences.

FOURTH: I give, devise, and bequeath the following items of personal property:

(a) To my good friend, Alice Jones, I give, devise, and bequeath the 1938 blue Hall Aladdin teapot;
(b) To my sister, JoAnn Smith, I give, devise, and bequeath the portrait of Rudolf Nureyev by Kenn Duncan, numbered 28/50.

It is advisable to be as specific as possible in distributing personal property. This again demonstrates testamentary capacity. Note that a gift can be general: "I leave my car to my sister, Jane Smith" is good for whatever car one owns at the time of one's death. However, since one may happen to own more than one car at the time of death, general bequests are not a very good idea. Be as specific as possible.

FIFTH: I give, devise, and bequeath the rest, residue, and remainder of my estate to my good friend and companion, Joe Doe, or if he should predecease me, then in equal shares to my mother and father, or if one of them shall predecease me, then to the survivor of them.

This article disposes of the remainder of the estate, called the residuary. This "catch-all" provision captures any property not specifically mentioned in the will, or which was mentioned but which had been bequeathed to a person no longer living. For instance, JoAnn Smith, the sister of the testator, may predecease him. There is no alternative beneficiary named with that particular bequest. Therefore, the portrait given her would be distributed as part of the residuary estate. JoAnn Smith's estate would not inherit the portrait unless she expired after the testator.

It adds to the shelf life of the will if there is an alternative beneficiary named as the residuary beneficiary. In that way, if the named residuary beneficiary dies before the testator, the will does not have to be redrafted; instead, the residuary estate will go to the person named as the alternative residuary beneficiary.

SIXTH: If any beneficiaries named in this will should contest the will for any reason and lose their challenge, they shall be treated as if they predeceased me for purposes of this my Last Will and Testament.

This is the in terrorem clause, making a will contest a gamble for any beneficiary named. The testator may not have a comfortable relationship with his parents and they may not be comfortable with the bulk of the estate being left to Joe Doe. However, if they contest the will, they will have an expensive undertaking and a poor chance of winning unless there is strong evidence of forgery, a lack of testamentary capacity, or influences over the testator that caused him to sign a will he would not have otherwise written. If the challengers lose in their bid, they lose everything left to them in the will.

SEVENTH: Should any beneficiary named in this, my Last Will and Testament, die in a common accident with me, then that person shall be treated as if he or she predeceased me.

This clause is an attempt to avoid the undesired effect of a beneficiary's estate inheriting a bequest, thereby delivering it to persons unintended and perhaps even unknown to the testator. For instance, while driving on a vacation the testator and Joe Doe have a car accident that is fatal to them both. If Joe Doe survives the testator for only a few moments and then dies himself, he would still stand to inherit. If he had no will, everything in his estate, including that which he inherited from the testator, would go to his next of kin. Therefore, to avoid that from happening, accident clauses are commonly put into wills. In some states, the accident clause is automatic by statute. Some people add a period of time, such as 30, 60, or 90 days that any beneficiary named in the will must outlive the testator.

EIGHTH: My executor shall have all of the powers vested in him/her by the State of _____.

This article authorizes an executor to do what is necessary to probate the estate. It may mean buying, selling, suing others, and, in essence, acting as the guardian over the estate. If special powers of some nature are to be transferred to an executor, then it can be done in this article.

Executed on this ___ day of_____ , 19___ , at Oakville, State of

_____.

Testator

There should be a minimum of three witnesses, generally speaking. Though many states only require two, where two are good, three are better. In that way, if, when the will goes to probate, a court wants to examine the witnesses, it has a better chance of locating at least two out of the pool of three.

POWERS OF ATTORNEY—OVERVIEW

As stated previously, a power of attorney delegates authority to another to do that which you can do yourself. A power of attorney comes in many forms, giving out a few or many powers or authorities, and lasting for a short time or for a very long time. Its design is up to you.

For instance, should you sign a financial power of attorney over your checking account to another person so that he or she can write checks, you may define it to be either broad or narrow in its scope:"I authorize John Doe to write my checks for me" or "I authorize John Doe to sign checks 101, 102, and 103 in amounts not to exceed $100 each only for the month of November 1996."

A power of attorney may concern your personal finances or it may be about business, authorizing another person to sign contracts for you in your place. It can also address medical decision making, authorizing another person to make medical decisions for you if you are incapable of making your own.

There are also different types of a power of attorney. For instance, a *durable power of attorney* means that the validity of the document is not affected by the subsequent disability of the signer. For example, if John Doe signs a power of attorney over to Jane Smith and is subsequently incapacitated, the document may no longer be valid. But if it is a durable power of attorney, the document retains its validity. A related type is called a *springing power of attorney*, which means that the document *only* takes effect upon your disability.

Be cautious with this legal instrument. A power of attorney is not to be given lightly but only under circumstances of extreme trust and where you can be in a position to revoke it or detect its misuse. There are many sad stories of people who have signed financial powers of attorney over to another individual only to find that the "friend" has departed with the bank account or other financial assets. The power of attorney is a document to be signed only after serious consideration and evaluation.

CONCLUSION

The process of writing a will and a power of attorney need not be complicated, expensive, or unpleasant. In fact, these instruments can mean something very special.

A will and a power of attorney can bring two people who aren't married as near as possible to the state of matrimony. This may not be a traditional method of entering matrimony, but since when have gays and lesbians been traditional? What a will and power of attorney offer is the power to force the law to respect this "outlaw" relationship. This experience can be very empowering. Some clients have will-signing parties that they treat as a ceremonies rather than morbid acts. In short, it is a way of declaring just how much power you have and how much you have to give.

Steps and Resources

- *Step*—Gather an inventory of your property, your family tree, all names and addresses of all parties concerned, and a description of your property.

- *Step*—Consider who the principal actors are in your will, who you trust to be executor and alternative executor for your estate or guardian for your children.
- *Resource*—For a referral to an attorney to write up a will, call the American Bar Association, your state or city bar association your local AIDS community-based organization, or alternative bar associations. Many cities have bar associations that are lesbian- and gay-oriented and may be resources for people in need of help. They are sometimes called by the name "Lesbian and Gay Bar Association" (or the reverse—"Gay and Lesbian") or, more often, "Bar Association for Human Rights." They may also have volunteer programs that assist those who cannot afford to hire an attorney.
- *Resource*—Choice in Dying — (formerly Concern for Dying and The Society for the Right to Die) is a national, nonprofit organization, best known for creating the first living will more than 25 years ago. The group will send one free, state-authorized advance directive to anyone who calls the toll-free number, 1-800-989-WILL (9455).

People with AIDS and Their Children

Providing for Custody

*The joys of parents are secret,
and so are their griefs and fears.*

Francis Bacon
Of Parents and Children

It is estimated that at least 30,000 children in the United States have lost one or both of their parents to AIDS. According to the Orphan Project of New York City, by the year 2000, the United States will have between 72,000 and 125,000 children who have been orphaned by AIDS, 30,000 of them in New York City alone.* In addition to the children who were born before their mothers were infected, the Centers for Disease Control estimates that between 1992 and the year 2000 a further 100,000 children will have been born to mothers with HIV. In 1993, for the first time, sexual contact became the predominant mode of transmission for women, surpassing drug use. Women, particularly women of color, are now rapidly increasing in AIDS diagnoses; in 1993 AIDS diagnoses among women increased by 9.8 percent as opposed to 2.5 percent among men. Taken together, these somber facts mean that the

---

*Worldwide, the number of children orphaned by AIDS is staggering. UNICEF estimates that there are 80,000 such orphans in Zambia alone and that by the year 2000, this number may swell to 625,000, or 11 percent of the children in that nation who are under the age of 15. In all of Africa, UNICEF estimates that the number of children orphaned will reach 5,000,000 by the end of the century.

special needs of the children of people with AIDS can only grow in magnitude.

The public mind connects the HIV epidemic with the plight of children with AIDS—babies who become infected at birth. While children with HIV are an important and tragic consequence of the epidemic, there is another large body of children—those who are affected but not infected by HIV. Though they have not necessarily contracted AIDS, their lives have nevertheless been destroyed by AIDS. Often, these children of parents with AIDS have had to act as a parent's caretaker, reversing roles with the parent by doing the shopping, picking up medications, making dinners, even buying diapers. They sometimes must bear the burden of their parent's condition alone, keeping it a secret out of a sense of shame and fear of the stigma that so often accompanies AIDS. And, to complicate matters further, these children often experience discrimination and their eventual placement is complicated by the fear of potential guardians, if uneducated about AIDS.

According to the Children's Rights Project of the Public Counsel of Los Angeles, only about half of the children orphaned by AIDS have a family member to take custody when their parent or parents are dead. Further, the Public Counsel asserts, about half of the mothers who die from AIDS do so without making any custody arrangements for their children.

BACKGROUND

From the beginning, experiences of children with AIDS in their families were troubled, to say the least. They not only lost their parent or parents but also found that they were shunned by other relatives, barred from school, and placed in undesirable foster care situations. Because AIDS so ravaged some communities in New York, many children lost an entire family in just a short time, a challenging situation from both a legal and practical perspective. One volunteer at the Gay Men's Health Crisis in New York remembers attending a woman in a hospital in the Bronx to write her will.

The attorney was called in near the end of the woman's life by the hospital social worker. She wanted to make a will to provide for the custody of her children. As it turned out, the children she wanted to provide for were not her children at all. Rather, they were her grandchildren, over whom she had received custody when their parents had died of AIDS two years before. Now, she too was dying of AIDS and the children were being orphaned for the second time in two years. Sadly, by the time the attorney arrived at the hospital, it was too late. The woman had entered a state of incoherency that made the writing of a will impossible. This type of situation, where children lose all family support, is not uncommon, and it is emotionally draining on all who are involved.

Mara Zeigler, L.C.S.W., of the Public Center in Los Angeles, works in the Children's Rights Project representing the interests of children who are faced with the complex set of circumstances that accompany the loss of a parent to HIV. "One of the things that doesn't make this simple," she says, "is the multigenerational nature of this disease. There is no other disease where the children have lost so many generations at the same time to this tragedy, and it goes against all developmental norms. Five year olds aren't supposed to go through that kind of loss in a span of two to five years." The first children affected in this way by the epidemic were often left without defenses. Until that point, the only alternative often left parents facing this circumstance was to write a will, expressing custodial preferences for their child. But this wasn't and isn't the ideal way to arrange for custody. In the will, expressing custody preferences may indicate the desire of the parent but may not be binding, particularly given the fact that much can change between the time the will is written and the time it is examined by the court. The designated guardian may have moved away, become ill, or expired. Further, pending the probate of the will, the child is placed in foster care. Some states allowed for a parent to arrange for the custody of children in the event of impending death, but doing so meant that the parent would give up custody of the child or children while still living and most parents did not want to do this. In addition, the process for examining the qualifications of an appointed guardian often did not begin until the death of the parent, which meant that the children were left in foster care until the new guardian was found to be suitable. This delay could place children in undesirable foster home situations at worst or, at best, in temporary and strange environments while most vulnerable in the wake of losing parent or parents. Moreover, if the designated guardian was found to be unfit, the children suffered permanent displacement.

As more children were impacted by AIDS, some states responded with laws that would create ways for parents to place their children while they were still living, to find a suitable guardian or guardians to bring the children into homes that welcomed them and were prepared for them. New York made provision for various kinds of custody arrangements, as did California. It became possible for parents to arrange for the custody of their children without actually giving up the children while they were living.

Legally, custody became easier to arrange but emotionally it is still a difficult and painful thing for any parent to do. Mara Zeigler has come to know firsthand how difficult it is for a parent to make these arrangements. Zeigler points out that the arrangements naturally go much more smoothly when they are made early but that families "still have to deal with denial, because many parents feel that in arranging custody, they are giving up." It is a difficult decision at best and, says Zeigler, "Parents usually aren't willing to go through this process unless they have gotten past their denial."

For the children, the realities of the situation are complex. Says Zeigler, "There may be any one or combination of sparring potential guardians, questions of benefits, issues of sexuality and drug use among parents, and the stigma of the disease." In addition, the family dynamic can be extremely difficult under the circumstances. "The whole issue of disclosure makes it very difficult. There are issues of fathers who have infected a spouse and children who are angry. For many of these kids, this is just one thing in a multiproblem setting."

For the parent with HIV, there is a wrenching decision to be made. But the cruelty of the situation has been somewhat softened by laws that make it possible to do the best thing for the child while not giving that precious child up.

OPTIONS FOR CUSTODY ARRANGEMENTS

While the motivation for a same-sex couple to write wills might be the empowerment inherent in getting the same rights as married couples, the motivation for a parent is often to protect the children. The options are more complicated for the parent. While gay couples sought this empowerment for the sake of becoming married in the eyes of the law, women with children were often driven to write a will for the purpose of stating their preferences for the custody of their children. Doing so allowed parents, through the means of their written will, to stand in court and state such preferences, even after they were deceased. While providing for children's custody is permissible in the will, it is not necessarily the surest method of seeing to the children's best interests and will merely serve as evidence of the parent's wishes. Where time permits, careful planning can best see to the needs of a child.

While custody arrangement for one's children may be the right thing to do and bring about a sense of peace as a result of attending to it, it is not by any means altogether easy. On the one hand, the parent is taking a positive step in exerting control and authority over what will happen to his or her child, acting with strength to protect the child. But in giving custody of one's children to another while still alive, or in designating another person as guardian, people may feel that they are giving up that which is most special in their lives, and the terrible emotional strain may interfere with their judgment.

Randye Retkin is the director of legal services at the Gay Men's Health Crisis in New York. A graduate of Howard Law School, her longstanding fascination with public interest law was satisfied when she came to GMHC to be the director in 1992. She and her husband have a small daughter, Emma. GMHC has had a legal department since 1984, when the department had a staff of one person, supported by approximately 20 volunteers. "Today," says Retkin, "we are 22 people, with 11 lawyers and 200 volunteer attorneys. We are a full-service law office for people with AIDS. We handle everything from wills and powers of attorney to debtor/creditor, landlord/tenant, insurance, discrimination, immigration, and family law. But a large part and a growing part in the past two years or more has been the family law portion."

The experience of Retkin's law office is varied slightly on the West Coast. At AIDS Project Los Angeles (APLA), the GMHC AIDS service counterpart, clients who are parents are predominantly gay males. But in New York, where the demographics of the epidemic have shifted much more rapidly than elsewhere and where there is a high concentration of women infected with HIV,* says Retkin, GMHC had to formulate a family law practice. "We were seeing more and more women coming into the agency. Now, between 15 and 20 percent of our clients at the Gay Men's Health Crisis are women, and 90 percent of the parents we see in our practice are women." And while that is not the experience of the West Coast, it appears that it will soon follow suit, with women increasing their profile in the epidemic from 2 percent of the cases six years ago to almost 11 percent in 1994.

The issues that face parents with AIDS are complex, legally, emotionally, and psychologically. While experiencing problems with their own health, parents must make emotionally trying decisions about the custody of their children, upon whom they may be depending for all levels of support. The situation forces parents not only to face their own mortality but also to acknowledge the painful reality that they cannot always be there for their child. Retkin acknowledges as a mother herself that "it is so wrenching

---

*The demographics of the epidemic have varied greatly between East Coast and West Coast. The existence of so many more injection drug users on the East Coast and the rapid spread of the epidemic among them facilitated the spread of AIDS into the heterosexual community in New York much more rapidly than in Los Angeles. Not only is injection drug use heavier on the East Coast but the existence of "shooting galleries," places where groups of people come together to shoot drugs, generally sharing needles, is much more common on the East Coast.

to think that you won't always be around for your child. Sometimes I see that parents think they are giving up when they make these decisions. But that's not true. Every parent, healthy or not, should make these decisions."

"The decision," she emphasizes, "is not just a legal decision, it is a practical one. Who is the best person to take care of my children?" Fortunately, there are ways for parents to arrange for custody of their children without necessarily giving them up during their lifetime.

Standby Guardianship

The assistance that can be offered to a parent is in the form of a standby guardianship, whereby a designated guardian is found for the child of the PWA. The guardianship is designated to a specific individual or a set of guardians but does not take effect until the biological parent is deceased. The designated new guardian may be a relative, but Retkin notes that in many cases, there is either no suitable relative, or worse, no one in the family left alive. In the case where there appears to be no available guardian, Retkin's department can refer the PWA to other nonprofit organizations that specialize in finding guardians for children. While few in number, such organizations are increasing. The situation is ideal if all the parties are in agreement, even if the PWA does not have someone in mind at the time he or she makes the decision. Retkin recalls such a situation.

"There was a client who had no one to leave a seven year old daughter with, and she felt that the relatives she had would not make good parents. She came to GMHC and was referred to a private placement agency. They linked the client up with a lawyer who wanted to adopt the daughter. The client executed a standby designation and started the adoption papers. The three of them spent time together, and when the client died, the daughter already knew her new mother, who then adopted her. The fact that she had made these arrangements was such a comfort to the client while she was in the hospital for the last time. It was the one thing she knew she could do. This," says Retkin, "was one good and loving mom."

If living in a state that permits standby guardianship, the key to success appears to be planning and involvement of all parties in the decision making process. Everyone may not, at first, agree. But to avert unforeseen interference by competing family members at the last moment, it is best that an agreement be attempted. Retkin recalls one client who had decided that she wanted friends to raise her child, when suddenly the client's brother decided instead that he wanted to raise the child himself. The parent/client didn't have the time left to go through the regular or standby guardianship proceedings. She was left expressing her guardianship preferences in her will, which was far less certain than going through an actual guardianship proceeding. In fact, a custody battle did not ensue in this case.

Above all, Retkin encourages people to talk to their children. "Talk to the children; even if they are young they know something is going on." She encourages her clients to work with mental health professionals to talk about disclosure issues. Retkin has seen the damage done to children with whom no one talked, for whom no one planned, and about whom no one could agree: "I have seen so many battles after the client has died and for the children to then be involved in the custody battle—that is as hard to take as being orphaned. It is traumatizing to the children twice, once by the parent's death and then by the disruption of their lives, not knowing what is going to happen to them."

Mara Zeigler and the Public Council Children's Rights Project approach their work differently than does GMHC, where the client is the parent. Before legislation was passed that arranged for joint guardianship, a parent would have to die before the custody of a child could be arranged, unless the parent gave up all custody rights with respect to his or her children. Now, a new law in California provides the mechanism for a joint guardianship, where custody is assured after death by virtue of the fact that the child's guardianship is shared with another. While guardianship is arranged for the future, the custody remains with the parent until such time as the parent either relinquishes control or passes away.

Temporary Guardianship

Standby guardianships and joint guardianships are becoming accepted as ways for a parent to designate a guardian for a child once the parent is deceased. However, one deficiency that remains, says Retkin, has to do with temporary guardianship, or placing a child with a caretaker only for a period of time. For most parents, the idea of giving up their children while they themselves are still alive is extremely difficult to accept. Yet, at the same time, as people with HIV, they have to deal with the episodic nature of the syndrome, of being well, then ill, then well again. Unfortunately, while parents can execute a document that provides temporary custody, it is not a document with the force of law in many states, though Florida and Pennsylvania allow it.

Temporary custody should have the force of law in order to provide a child's temporary custodian with the same decision-making rights as the parent. Without it, the child can be put at risk for injury and the temporary guardian can be helpless. A temporary guardian is nothing more than a baby sitter unless the position of temporary guardian is supported by a law. And a baby-sitter has no power, should a child suffer an accident where medical attention is needed, to make decisions on behalf of the child. Likewise, the temporary guardian cannot make necessary medical decisions unless the temporary custody arrangement has the force of law. A physician or hospital treating the child may want to listen to the temporary guardian but has no legal basis for doing so and can legally only turn to the biological parent. If the biological parent is indisposed because of illness, the child may be the one to suffer. Temporary custody, when provided for by statute, allows the temporary guardian to make decisions regarding medical attention and schooling that may be important and essential to the child's well-being, and a treating physician can then adhere to the decisions made by the temporary guardian.

With the potential increase in the United States of children orphaned by AIDS, family law is one of the fastest growing legal aspects of the epidemic. The legalities are relatively simple, but the realities are not. In states where there is a high incidence of AIDS, state legislatures need to take note. Even where HIV incidence is not high, temporary guardianship arrangments for parents with cancer or other life-threatening illnesses should be sanctioned by law.*

"The legal aspects of this could be explained in a few minutes," says Retkin, "but there is an emotional piece that I have never felt before in the practice of law. It is so emotionally wrenching to make a decision like this about your children, and I really give parents the utmost credit who walk into my office and actually put their plans into effect."

Like so many issues discussed in this book, there are psychosocial ramifications to planning for one's own children in the wake of one's death, making the law respect one's otherwise "illegitimate" gay relationship, or the simple act of writing a will. It is perhaps important to bear in mind that making the decision to go forward is a positive one. It is an effort by you to take authority over a difficult situation and to exert as much control as possible. Whatever the circumstances, people feel better when they are in control. Says Mara Zeigler, "They all feel a peace of mind."

Steps and Resources

Child custody arrangements vary widely from state to state. Some of the highest HIV/AIDS incidence states have enacted legislation to make custody arrangements more humane and considerate, though California only did so in 1994 when it enacted a new Joint Guardianship Law.

*Many people assume that women with AIDS are concentrated only in large metropolitan areas. However, the proportion of women with AIDS increased from 4 percent in 1984 to 15 percent in 1993. Much of the growth among women is taking place in rural America, particularly in the South. With respect to HIV, Georgia reported that 70 women in Atlanta were known to have given birth in 1991, but 94 women who were HIV-positive gave birth elsewhere in the state.

If you have children, you should become familiar with your options right away. Because children are involved, psychosocial issues are extremely important here. A parent may need help in deciding how and when to tell a child about HIV, about being gay, or about other adult matters that could place a burden on the child. Therefore, in seeking help, you may want to find resources that will help you with both the legal and the psychosocial issues that can arise.

The first step is to understand what options are available so that you will be able to choose wisely and to explain your decisions to your children. With so many different state laws, it is helpful that a resource in Washington, D.C., can help you learn what laws apply to your situation and assist you in securing the help you need. The Child Welfare League of America assists parents who have a terminal illness. The telephone number is 202-638-2952 and by contacting the league, you can find what local resources are available to you. The league has also produced a booklet, available through the Centers for Disease Control National AIDS Clearinghouse at 800-458-5231.

In addition, gather all the information you have about your child:

- Medical records
- Birth certificates, Social Security cards
- Bank accounts
- A family tree

In addition, you might talk to people locally:

- Speak to the social worker in the hospital where you receive care
- Call the family court and ask the clerk of the court for information about what options may be open to you
- Look locally for any Children's Rights Projects; call Legal Aid or any children's societies for information.

3

Owing . . . The American Dream

A creditor is worse than a master
for a master owns only your person;
a creditor owns your dignity,
and can belabour that.

Victor Hugo
Les Misérables

The area of finance is a metaphor for all of AIDS in that it represents one of the areas most out of control for a person living with HIV. It is a metaphor for the immune system itself. There are few options for restoring it. It is likely to be a great source of depression and anxiety to a PWA. Dollars and resources, like T cells, can become fewer with the passage of time. It is a problem that exists for nearly everyone with HIV, despite the extent of personal resources they may have at the outset of the challenge to their health.

The country has thrived on a system of sustained debt. Americans have had access to large credit lines that, like the nation itself, allow them to spend more money than they have, making payments that are relatively small over a great period of time. People who cannot spend $10,000 in cash can charge $10,000 worth of merchandise, paying $150 per month. They can keep charging as long as they do not surpass their credit ceiling. As long as the payments are made, there are no problems, other than the fact that the debtor is paying large sums in interest payments. And this is the way most Americans have become accustomed to living. This system, of course, works smoothly until the payments are missed.

Most people become depressed when faced with a situation or situations that they cannot control. Nothing in this chapter or in this book can completely restore all areas of control to a PWA. However, in the area of finances especially, it is important to keep the PWA from becoming victimized. Loss of finances, inability to pay debt, loss of purchasing power, and even having a home threatened by foreclosure or by eviction can divert a PWA's attention from where it needs to be, focused on his medical condition and his battle against the virus. And the loss of one's livelihood and ability to pay for necessities is more than symbolic of a loss of control; it is a constant and daily reminder.

BACKGROUND

It is probably difficult to pinpoint when our society became addicted to credit but it is prudent to recall that there was a time in America when people paid cash for almost everything they purchased. It was a simple equation. If you didn't have the money, you didn't get the merchandise. No percentage rates, no annual fees. Just a simple and straight cash transaction. The exception, of course, was for real estate, where you could borrow money from a bank and pay it off over time through a mortgage. Or, in colonial days, you could raise capital for a business through investors. But for the average John and Jane Doe, credit was not something readily available.

America and commercial transactions necessarily became more complicated with the advent of the Industrial Revolution. The pace of the economy and the diversity of goods made purchase by credit a very desirable thing. Someone then decided that installment contracts would be a good idea. This was an instrument, which the creditor and borrower both signed, that said that you could take home the merchandise and pay it off by installment. If, however, you failed to meet your payments on the installment contract, then you forfeited the merchandise back to the seller. This became a common way to purchase large appliances or furniture. This type of purchase through an installment contract is what is known as a *secured transaction*. That means that the security of the lender is tied up in the goods that are purchased. If there is a failure to pay for the goods, then they can be taken away. In short, the promise to pay by the borrower is secured by the goods themselves.

Credit cards specific to the stores eventually gave way to mass credit cards, which allowed one to make purchases at almost any store or restaurant anywhere in the world. The development of the magnetic strip and the increasing sophistication of computers made installment contracts unnecessary, except in the purchase of an automobile. Plastic revolutionized the purchasing power of the American family and of debtor and creditor law. With credit cards, the notion of a secured transaction flew out the window. Credit card purchases are, for the most part, *unsecured transactions*. This means that the only thing that is securing the promise to pay by the borrower is the promise itself. The promise becomes a commodity in and of itself. A failure to pay does not result in a credit card company coming and repossessing the goods themselves; rather, they have a right to sue you for the money, and the value of your promise to pay erodes, as this effort by the lender is noted in your credit rating.

What had historically begun as an occasional simple installment plan for most consumers now became a credit empire. Now, millions in our society live part of this American Dream. People who live in the United States are more debt-ridden and save less than people in most other developed nations. It is a system that has worked for most people, or at least worked in the respect that they have increased their present purchasing power by mortgaging some part of their financial future, not unlike, some would argue, the example set by our national government. It is a choice that is available to most people, and to some degree, it is exercised by all. Credit is such an addiction, and even a necessity, that one can often spot flyers or credit services that will get you a credit card in your name despite a bad credit history or prior bankruptcy. There is one serious threat, however, that stands out above all others when a person undertakes a large debt load—disability.

This was particularly true when AIDS first manifested itself in the early 1980s. Gay men in large metropolitan areas were the first and hardest hit. In the first few years of the epidemic, gay men comprised over 90 percent of the diagnosed cases of AIDS, as compared to today, when the national average is closer to 61 percent. Before 1985, there was no HIV antibody test, and an AIDS diagnosis came without warning. One day a person felt fine, the next week he was in the hospital. Without the benefit of today's better medical treatment of persons with opportunistic infections, people died more quickly. In large numbers, gay men, many of whom had been affluent, suddenly found themselves unable to work because of their illness. Without income, and with sharply increased medical expenses, they were unable to pay their bills. In large part, this indebtedess became inconsequential because of premature death. Many or most did not have disability insurance.

While that was the typical milieu of the early 1980s, by the mid-1980s the scene began to change. Especially in East Coast cities, there was a large demographic swing in the epidemic so that women, particularly poor minority urban women, were becoming diagnosed in greater numbers.* In general, persons of color began to show up in the demographic profile of the caseload as a greater and greater share, until their representation in the makeup of AIDS cases outweighed their numerical profile in the general population.† In increasingly greater numbers, socially and economically challenged persons were affected and infected by AIDS. In short,

*The Centers for Disease Control reported in 1992 that, while it took eight years to diagnose the first 100,000 cases of AIDS, the second 100,000 cases occured within only 26 months. Differences in the first 100,000 from the second 100,000 were apparent, with a 44 percent increase in heterosexual transmissions, with 24 percent of the newer cases being among drug users as compared to 20 percent in the first 100,000; with only 55 percent of the cases occurring among gay or bisexual men (a decline from the 60 percent profile in the first 100,000 cases); and with a jump for African Americans from 27 percent to 31 percent and for Hispanics from 15 percent to 17 percent.

†The National Commission on AIDS reported in 1993 that African Americans and Latinos comprised 46 percent of all people known to have been diagnosed with AIDS in the United States, despite the fact that they comprised only 21 percent of the American population.

while we at one time viewed AIDS through a lens that examined how the disease *made people poor*, it became necessary to flip the lens and look at how AIDS began to *impact the poor*.

In either case, the rights of creditors versus debtors are largely unchanged. On the one hand, a person who is financially downwardly mobile as a result of having symptomatic HIV infection may be relatively inexperienced in dealing with the system and may find himself or herself open to wanton threats of creditors and prone to a knee-jerk reaction of declaring bankruptcy. On the other hand, people who have always been socioeconomically deprived and unable to pay a large stack of bills may find that they now have some legal protections that they did not have before. In any case, however, for people who are being squeezed financially while at the same time having to count their T cells and guard their immune system, debtor/creditor problems can be an unbearable obstacle. But there are solutions to many of the problems.

WHEN THERE IS NOWHERE LEFT TO TURN

Tom Barnes is a staff attorney with AIDS Project Los Angeles, the second-largest AIDS service organization in the nation. The legal services program was begun in 1991 and works to assist people in estate planning and in debtor/creditor situations. It is his job to help people find the solutions that are best for a person with these kinds of problems. "It is a very scary thing for people," he says, "and about half of what I do involves anxiety reduction for my clients."

When faced with debtor/creditor crises, it is important to realize that you are not without options and that there are actually several good reasons to do something about your situation rather than nothing, hoping that the matter will take care of itself.

First, it is important to maintain a good credit rating as far as possible, as the credit may be needed during the course of illnesses one may face.

Secondly, creditors want their money. It means harassing telephone calls and endless letters and can result in adding a great deal of stress to one's life.

And thirdly, doing something about it helps to make someone a "person with AIDS" as opposed to an "AIDS victim." The psychosocial motivation to get some ease from the financial strain goes beyond the obvious desire to keep creditors from calling. To any degree for any person with AIDS, getting some control over what is going on in one's life is important. Just as debt can be viewed as a metaphor for what is happening with the immune system, getting some control over creditors is a metaphor for controlling all of the other effects of HIV disease. The more control that people can establish over their lives, the better they feel. That is particularly true of people with AIDS. Therefore, whether a downwardly mobile middle-class gay man from West Hollywood or a Latina from the Bronx, every PWA has the same desire to gain control over his or her life, and fighting the fight may be just as important as winning it. There are many options open, and it helps to have someone like Tom Barnes to help.

Bankruptcy

For many people who feel hopeless about their financial situation, a knee-jerk reaction is "I want to declare bankruptcy." This is *a* way, not *the* way to deal with financial distress. Technically, bankruptcy is a means by which an individual or a business can declare insolvency and seek protection of the law from creditors, either to get an entire new start or to have time to reorganize their finances. With individuals, bankruptcy is usually declared in order to get a new start; with businesses, it is to reorganize.

The laws of bankruptcy keep creditors at bay. Any lawsuits pending against you are halted. Attachments and garnishments stop. It is as if a protector lands between you and your creditors, and none can pass. It sounds like a good deal. But nothing comes for nothing. There is a price to pay for bankruptcy.

In order to declare bankruptcy, you must have time and patience. It is not an overnight process and can require several months' worth of time.

- You will need to pay an attorney to assist you, and you will need to pay filing fees to the court.
- In addition, you are required to have less than $2500 in liquid assets (not including your automobile).
- You must show that you have not have given preferential treatment to any single creditor over another.
- You must have been unable to pay any of your creditors for a period of six months.
- You cannot have declared bankruptcy within the past seven years.

The process will involve an examination of your history with your creditors by the court, and any of your creditors may challenge your petition. If you own much property beyond a home in which you reside, it may be subject to liquidation so that any amounts therefrom can be used to satisfy your creditors. Likewise, any investments you may have made toward your future are also subject to scrutiny and possible liquidation. There will be a great deal of scrutiny to determine if, in fact, you can pay your bills but are merely unwilling to do so.

Tom Barnes recently helped a person with AIDS declare bankruptcy. His client had been earning $100,000 per year. With the onset of his AIDS condition, he was no longer able to work and his income plummeted. At the same time and also as a result of his disability, his expenses rose. Prior to his disability, he had been carrying credit card debt, which together amounted to almost $30,000, which was all *unsecured* debt. He was an appropriate candidate for bankruptcy because he had substantial debt and could not pay it, no longer being able to meet the mimimum monthly payments due on the cards. None of his debt was owed to his hospital or medical provider. While he had owned real estate, he made a gift of it to someone else. This gift was uncomplicated because he had no real equity in the real estate. He had been leasing an automobile, which he had to turn in and discharge his debt. He was an appropriate bankruptcy candidate because

- His debt was substantial

- He owned no property
- He did not owe his medical provider
- He was not declaring bankruptcy against anything other than unsecured transactions

Note that if Tom's client had owed his medical provider, Tom might not have recommended bankruptcy. "This is a big issue when people are still going to a doctor or hospital whom they are declaring bankruptcy against, because the doctor or hospital may stop treating them." This is not the only situation Tom warns clients about. "It can be quite hard to get an apartment or a credit card, or open a bank account after declaring bankruptcy. Of course, bad credit can also affect your ability to get any of these things, but not as much as having a bankruptcy on your record."

In contrast to the client making $100,000, Barnes recounts a recent experience with another client. This man was the head of his household and had become disabled because of his AIDS diagnosis. Prior to his disability, he and his wife had purchased some needed appliances for their kitchen, most notably a stove. Because they could not get a bank credit card either because of income level or credit history, the couple purchased the stove on time from the store, meaning the transaction was a *secured* one. Now the couple could no longer meet the payments on the installment agreement and stood to have the stove and other appliances repossessed by the store. They were not good candidates for bankruptcy since the transaction was secured and since the total amount of debt was actually not very high. The couple hoped that their situation might change the next year with higher social security payments that would allow them to meet a monthly installment agreement. Tom Barnes had, therefore, undertaken the task of renegotiating with the store. The caveat to this story, warns Barnes, is that many store-owned credit cards may be considered secured transactions, thereby securing the debt with the actual merchandise, rather than unsecured, as with a bank credit card, where the debt is secured only by a promise to pay.

A further word of caution regarding bankruptcy—if you are seeking to declare it because of insurmountable debts due the government for back taxes and/or student loans, the relief you seek will be more complicated. Only those taxes delinquent over three years may be discharged in bankruptcy and student loans may be discharged, but there will be several additional requirements beyond a normal bankruptcy. It may be required that you undertake specific applications to the appropriate agencies for hardship cases due to disability. To do this, you should seek the professional help of an attorney through a legal services program available to persons without the ability to pay for their own lawyer. This may be through legal aid societies or your local AIDS service organization.

You may not be appropriate for declaring bankruptcy for a number of reasons. Your debt may not be great enough. "You only get one shot every seven years," says Barnes, referring to the number of times you are allowed to declare bankruptcy. "You have to make sure it's worth it." Or, if you have debt that is secured by the property, you lose the property if you stop paying, even if you file bankruptcy. Simply put, you may not need to go through bankruptcy even though it seems like the only way out.

If Not Bankruptcy, What?

Bankruptcy is the most draconian of ways to deal with the problem of financial distress. To understand other options, it is first important to understand what one's rights are and what the relationship really is between debtor and creditor.

A creditor has a right to the money you owe him. Many people who are disabled offer the excuse, "I'm disabled, I'm sick, now I can't pay." True as that may be, the reason for nonpayment is of little concern to the creditor. When you filled out a credit application, you signed a credit agreement. In that agreement, the credit company agreed to loan you money to make purchases or give you cash advances in exchange for your promise to pay. Nowhere in that contract does it say that if you cannot pay because of a very good reason everything is fine and the creditor will just write it off. A creditor has a right to go after the money by taking a number of actions.

First, the credit company will send those friendly reminders advising you, in case you didn't know, that your payment hasn't been received. Then, if payment is still not received, that credit will no longer be extended. The creditor may then hand the matter over to its collections department, which will take to calling you on a regular basis to inquire whether or not you are going to pay. Finally, after a period of several months, the collections department will move to file a suit and you will receive a summons and complaint.

When a Debtor Is Sued

A summons and complaint is the kickoff to a lawsuit. In this case it is issued at the behest of the creditor, the person to whom you owe the money, to gain satisfaction from the debtor, you. In return, a summons and complaint demands an answer from the defendant.

Many people seem to believe that if they can avoid the service of a summons and complaint, then they will be able to buy time and find some way of getting out of their plight. However, service of the summons and complaint in a credit case in many states will occur by certified mail. Ignoring the mail will only necessitate the service of the summons and complaint in some other fashion. Ultimately, unless you can pack all of your assets and go to another planet, service is difficult to avoid altogether. It is probably easier on you and everyone concerned to go pick up the certified mail, so that you can begin doing something about your problem immediately, rather than letting it hang over your head. Denial will not make the matter go away.

The summons and complaint will be a form document that will be short and to the point, written in language that sounds as though it were written by an artificial life form.

1. That the credit card company, MasterPassport, is a duly licensed credit card company in the state of Spottsylvania;
2. That the defendant, John Doe, currently residing at 23 Elm Street, Anywhere, U.S.A., opened a credit account with

Plaintiff on January 15, 1994 and that Defendant currently has an outstanding balance of $5454.54;

3. That under the terms of said agreement, Defendant is to submit to Plaintiff monthly installments on any outstanding balance;

4. That Defendant has not submitted an installment payment since December 15, 1995 and Defendant is five (5) months in arrears on said payments;

5. That Plaintiff is duly owed the entire sum of the balance plus court costs.

This complaint now demands an answer. Your answer is filed with the court and responds to each numbered allegation contained in the complaint. If a defendant does not respond at all, then a default judgment occurs in favor of the plaintiff, meaning the creditor automatically wins. If, in fact, a debtor defendant owes money and isn't paying it then when the defendant puts in an answer, he will necessarily have to admit the truth of the allegations contained in the complaint. Once an answer is filed by the defendant, then the court will set a court date and arguments will be heard for either side. As mentioned before, being disabled is not a defense. Therefore, in all likelihood, by putting in an answer to the complaint and going to court with the defense of being sick, you will lose just as if you did not put in an answer at all. Either they will win automatically or they will win when you go to court. In short, they win.

The fact *that* they win may not be as important as *what* they win, however. In the situation where a person is employed and owes money and is sued by a creditor or creditors, then by going to court those creditors may get a judgment against the defendant. That judgment tells the defendant that he must pay, which presumably the defendant already knows. If the defendant refuses to pay, then the creditors may go to court and get the judgment *enforced*. If the debtor owns real estate, a lien might be put on it, meaning that when the property is sold, the debt must be satisfied out of the proceeds of the sale. If the debtor is working, his or her wages may be garnished. No more than 25 percent of wages can be garnished.

If there is one creditor, then 25 percent may be garnished; if there are 10 creditors, still only 25 percent can be garnished.

When a Poor and Disabled Person Is Sued

Off the top of his head, Tom Barnes estimates that nearly 90 percent of his clients are "judgment-proof," meaning that the someone may go to court, sue them, get a judgment against them, and then be unable to enforce it because there is nothing to enforce it against. The case of a person with HIV is often this: the financial network, if there was one, has been eroding faster than the immune system; long standing bills on revolving charge cards exist; the person is no longer working, is on private disability, living off savings, or has applied for government benefits that won't even meet rent payments. Or, as AIDS impacts more and more people who are economically challenged, the person with HIV may have been in debtor/creditor distress all of his life, and the only difference now is that he is disabled.

In either case, when a creditor sues the disabled, all of the above actions may ensue; however, when it gets to the point of judgment, there may be nothing the creditor can do. If you are not working, there are no wages to attach. If you have no real property, there is nothing upon which to put a lien. If you are getting government benefits, they cannot be garnished like wages. The one action open to the creditor is to put a lien on a bank account; however, defendants may simply close their bank accounts as a precaution and operate without one, especially since they do not have a great deal of income. The creditor may be barred from putting such a lien on the account if the money in it is derived from disability payments. In short, while disability is not a defense to a lawsuit for nonpayment of the money owed, the fact that AIDS has already taken the money a person may have had may leave the creditor holding the bag. By the end of the process, the creditor has sent you letters, paid a collection agency or lawyer to draw up a summons and complaint, filed it with the court—all to get from the court a piece of paper that says that the debtor owes the money, which is what was had in the first place. If a debtor with AIDS doesn't have any assets and has no income, then he or she is what is termed "judgment proof." You are likely to have this status if

- you own no real estate
- you have no job and no income other than disability income
- you have no assets that could be attached, including bank accounts

Judgment proof status is not something that should be abused or taken lightly. But it is a reality. Tom Barnes states, "Most of my clients want to pay their bills and think about a way to try to work this out. They would pay their bills if they could." When they can't, Tom advises them on what they can do and how they might avoid bankruptcy while at the same time easing the burden of their debt, though judgment proof status doesn't keep someone from being sued. "Judgment proof status," warns Tom Barnes, "is a lot like being bullet proof. Just because it's there doesn't mean someone isn't going to shoot at you; it just means that it has no effect." In essence, the disabled person with no assets is like Teflon when it comes to enforcing a judgment. The old cliché "You can't squeeze blood from a stone" comes to life.

There are ways to save wear and tear on everyone's nerves. As mentioned, declaring bankruptcy is not a fun process. Neither is being sued. But there are other possibilities that exist that can and should be explored.

Many credit card companies, for instance, carry insurance policies on a person to cover the possibility of the debtor's becoming disabled, especially if it is a gold charge card. A debtor should check to see if there are any such disability policies connected with any of his or her charge cards or bank lines of credit.

Even if there are no such possibilities, there is still room for negotiation. In the early days of the health crisis, banks and charge card companies were not terribly inclined to take part in any dialogue regarding the status of the debtor. With increasing incidence of AIDS-related defaults, there was a shift in this willingness. Legal services programs serving people with AIDS devised letters for their clients that were sent to all creditors advising the creditor of the disabled status of the person with AIDS. It would state flatly that the person was in all likelihood judgment proof and that further efforts would be useless. At first, companies ignored these letters. But as the numbers swelled and the companies got more and more of these letters, they began to listen and would often be willing to cease and desist collection efforts. Tom Barnes indicates that he has only had three creditors in the past year who have been noncompliant in response to these letters. "The only issue with large credit card banks," he says, "is that they are gigantic, and it can take time to work things through the bureaucracy for them to make a decision. So I usually send out the letters and have them call me and after two or three times, the matter is resolved."

There is also an increased willingness on the part of the companies to negotiate. If it is at all possible to do so, the debtor should consider a negotiated settlement. This would involve a lower payment and perhaps a freezing of the rate of interest on the account in exchange for a monthly payment. For a debtor with some assets and few debts, this would be a very sound action.

However, not everyone can pay even a little. In the mid 1980s, a man named David in Manhattan was having creditor problems. He did not have a great deal of debt. His credit card companies were written and one responded with an offer to cut off the interest from the debt and to accept small monthly payments of $25 on a balance that was $5000. While this seemed an extremely reasonable offer, David was relying on federal entitlements of $575 each month to support himself. He had no savings left. He had no private disability policy. He lived alone in an apartment that cost $600 per month. And the same week that the offer came from the creditor, David, who had become blind as a result of an opportunistic infection, found that his food stamps were being cut. As attractive as the offer was from the credit card company, there was no way David was going to find the $25 each month to pay it.

David was as judgment proof as they come. Creditors could go to court and sue him, but it would merely be an exercise for their computers in generating paperwork because they would get nothing. Still, David did not need to be getting harassing telephone calls from creditors. The only surefire way to stop that is through bankruptcy or by paying the bill. There are limits with respect to the nature and timing of the calls creditors make to your home and business, but the company does have a right to call and ask for its money as long as you owe it.

An excellent resource is consumer credit agencies, which are formed to offer advice and counsel to those in consumer credit stress. They are usually nonprofit agencies who may be able to guide you through the turbulent waters of trying to figure out what you can do, given your particular situation.

The Permanent Debt—Rent

There is one other person who often doesn't get his regular payment during a time of financial stress brought about as a result of disability. The landlord has a contract with a tenant called a lease. Oftentimes, as with credit, people may naively assume that the fact that they have acquired a disability means that they can't be sued. While we do not live in the bad times described in the books of Charles Dickens, they are not all that much better, either.

The impact of HIV on the individual is financially so great that there are estimates that up to half of persons diagnosed with AIDS must relocate within a year of the diagnosis to a less expensive living situation. As the demographics of the epidemic shift to more economically challenged individuals, this may become an even greater percent.

The beginning of a lawsuit for eviction for nonpayment of rent is similar to that of the debtor–creditor action, in that it begins with a summons and complaint. The relief sought by the landlord is that the tenant pay back rent and vacate the premises. Of course, court costs are tacked on.

Courts are not fond of evicting people, and there may be several opportunities to delay an eviction. However, what is clear is that unless a method of payment is found, eviction will occur. A person is not forgiven rent because he or she has AIDS.

The options for people depend largely on the resources that are available in a particular community for people with AIDS or disabilities. In New York, the city welfare department has been useful, while in other cities, there may be private charity resources, state funds, or other municipal agencies that can be of help in the situation.

A landlord has no obligation to allow a person to stay without paying rent because of disability. Once rent is not paid, a person is given several methods of warning and then will be brought into court; if rent cannot be produced, eviction will occur. However, if there are resources to assist the disabled tenant in paying the back rent, then the strategy should be to stall that court date as long as possible while lining up any assistance that might be available.

This goal can be accomplished in the most legitimate of ways. If, for instance, an application is being made to federal entitlement programs after a person is newly diagnosed as having a disability, there may be a back payment due to the person with AIDS, dating back to the time of the disability. Whether this is the case, or a city or private agency is prepared to assist with the payment of back rent, the person with AIDS/tenant/defendant will need to deal with the action that is pending in court to evict him.

An eviction proceeding often begins with a notice to the tenant that a proceeding is going to be brought against him if rent is not paid. The term for this notice is usually three days, but it can vary by jurisdiction. This three-day notice is not a notice stating that in three days eviction will occur, as it is often construed to be. Eviction can only occur after there has been a court case.

As with the debtor/creditor summons and complaint, the petition for relief by the landlord will contain a series of allegations. It is necessary for the tenant/defendant to file an answer to the complaint. In many jurisdictions, this answer to the allegations can be filed with the clerk of the court orally, and the clerk records the response to the allegations. Whether in writing or orally, once it is done, a court date will be set. The court date will be within a matter of days.

On the summons and complaint appear the name and address and telephone number of the attorney for the landlord. If the person with AIDS is represented by an attorney, which is, of course, preferable, then the defendant's attorney may call the plaintiff's attorney and ask that he stipulate to a changed date for the court date. This sort of delay is common among attorneys, and, as a matter of professional courtesy, a first delay is usually consented to. The parties will stipulate to the change date in a notice to the court in writing. If, by the time the court date is arriving, the person with AIDS has still not received the financial assistance applied for, another delay can be sought from the opposing attorney. A second one may in fact be agreed to, but if it is not, then the person with AIDS or his representative will have to go to court on the day the case is to be called. When it is called, the defendant can ask for another adjournment of the court date due to the circumstances of the application for assistance that will provide funds for the payment of the rent by a date certain, making the entire court case moot. Proof of the application for assistance may be necessary to furnish and a copy of the application should be available for the court to examine.

CONCLUSION

In short, being in debt is not the best idea, though it is tough to avoid, especially when the government sets such a good example for us. Debt is a way of life, and the management of credit does not always foresee the possibility of disability. Or, as AIDS impacts more and more economically challenged people, credit problems around people with AIDS will abound. To add to the problem, the fact of the matter is that for many, living off credit is the only alternative in the face of medications that are not covered by insurance or Medicaid or by any national health-care coverage.

But when in debt and disabled, a person does not need to feel further victimized by a system that is insensitive to the fact that one has become disabled or lost income due to the challenges of HIV.

It is possible to take some control over the situation, and there are options. Concentration for the person with HIV needs to be on health care, and the distractions of nasty creditors should not get in the way of that priority. While there are no complete remedies, there are ways to assume authority and control.

Steps and Resources

- *Step*—check credit cards and lines of credit for the possibility that there is a policy of disability insurance connected with them
- *Step*—find the resources available in your area for credit and financial counseling
- *Step*—renegotiate with your creditors
- *Step*—determine whether you are "judgment proof"
- *Step*—determine whether you are a good candidate for bankruptcy
- *Resource*—AIDS community based organizations
- *Resource*—consumer credit groups
- *Resource*—legal aid societies

4

What's Owed to You

Entitlements

Taxes are what we pay for civilized society.

Oliver Wendell Holmes, Jr.
Compania de Tabacos v. Collector
275 U.S. 87, 100

There is a series of "safety nets" constructed and paid for through our government and, hence, by our taxes. These safety nets have been constructed over the years to protect the people in our society who, for one reason or another, have become financially vulnerable due to an inability to work because of disability. Given shifts in the political landscape, the government commitment to this safety net may vary enormously.

Some of the terms for this network of safety nets are familiar to all of us yet carry little specific meaning: social security, Medicaid, Medicare, welfare. For many, these terms are vague because they are systems that, generally, we did not think we would need to utilize until old age, if then. Medicare, after all, is what one's grandparent may have but not a thirty year old. Some of the programs offered by the federal government are reactions to the pain and suffering caused by the Great Depression, while others were formulated or enhanced greatly by the concept of the Great Society, envisioned under the administration of President Lyndon Johnson.

In addition to federal programs, depending on where one lives there may be state efforts in ensuring the needs of its citizens. States also may be influential in the way that federal programs are administered in the state, creating differences in funding levels among the states. In some cases, state programs will interact jointly with federal programs, as with Medicaid, causing there to be a great variance on a state by state basis in the benefits that may be available under that program.

The entire spectrum of benefits available in the public sector presents a complicated set of challenges to people who need to access it. Assistance in making applications is desirable and may be available to you at your nearest AIDS service organization. Hospital social work departments may also be a resource. Though they will be focusing their efforts on people who are patients and may not be open to the general public, they may be able to offer a referral for where assistance may be obtained.

As with any of the challenges posed in these pages, however, the key to obtaining all of the benefits to which one is entitled is preparation.

BACKGROUND

Early in the epidemic, with HIV as a "new" disease, the safety net was not very good at supporting people with AIDS because it was not clear to some government officials that HIV/AIDS was a "disability" within the meaning of the laws that authorized the various programs. AIDS appeared as a crisis very quickly, but government bureaucracy, by its nature, is not known for its speed.

The situation was further complicated by the stigma of AIDS. When the first cases of AIDS were diagnosed and people applied for federal entitlements, workers in the offices would refuse to handle AIDS applications, fearing they would contract the disease by processing the papers. Some reactions were extreme. In the early 1980s in Los Angeles, one social security worker set her dress on fire after she had provided service to a person with AIDS. Time has not necessarily brought about great change, as seen in 1995 when secret service personnel, out of fear of contagion, wore rubber gloves to greet gay and lesbian elected officials visiting the White

House. Because people and a system were not ready to cope, people died before they could receive their benefits, or would receive nothing for months and then suddenly get a check for several hundreds or thousands of dollars, paying them back to the time of their disability but arriving only after months of impoverishment. In addition, because people were diagnosed later in the syndrome than they are today and because physicians were not very good at treating opportunistic infections, people applying for benefits often would not get an award of benefits until after they had died. In short, the system simply was not nimble or pliable enough to respond to what was going on with the burgeoning needs of people caught in the epidemic. While at first it was difficult to get social security to recognize AIDS as a disability, once it did the problems did not end. When AIDS was first recognized by the Centers for Disease Control and Prevention (CDC), there were two levels of HIV infection in addition to the condition of AIDS.

1. HIV positive meant that you had tested positive for the antibody that causes AIDS but were symptom-free.
2. AIDS Related Complex (ARC)—a term has since become antiquated in the natural history of the epidemic—was very important in 1985.
3. "Full-blown AIDS"—an unfortunate term—signaled that one's immune system had been depleted to the point where certain opportunistic infections were manifest.

ARC was a state of being between being HIV positive and having "full-blown" AIDS. At the time, the CDC had a narrower definition of what comprised an AIDS diagnosis. A diagnosis meant that you had a positive HIV test coupled with one of several opportunistic infections. However, during this time, while people with AIDS were able to gain access to entitlement programs because a disability status was presumed to accompany the condition of AIDS, people with ARC had the arduous task of setting forth proof that their ARC diagnosis was, in fact, disabling. This was an extremely inequitable situation, often resulting in the fact that a person could be classified as a person with AIDS, and thus get benefits, because of the existence of one Kaposi's Sarcoma lesion on the body, while a person with chronic and disabling diarrhea or other ARC condition might be much more ill and much less able to work. The person with ARC either had to jump through arduous hoops to get benefits, or, as was often likely, would not get benefits at all.

In 1987, the definition was expanded again to include more opportunistic infections, bringing the number to 23 different clinical conditions comprising an AIDS diagnosis. However, while this change did result in greater numbers of those with ARC being considered disabled, there were still people with severe symptomatic HIV infection who were left out in the cold. Women particularly suffered as the gynecological manifestations of HIV disease were left off the list, thus effectively barring assistance, or at least making it extremely difficult for women with medical conditions that today we recognize as AIDS.

To some extent, this identity crisis still pervades the issues around public benefits. Only in 1991 did the definition once again change to reflect a positive HIV test coupled with a status of fewer then 200 T-helper cells or coupled with one of 26 opportunistic infections, having added pulmonary tuberculosis, recurrent pneumonia, and invasive cervical cancer. For all intents and purposes, at this time the status of ARC ceased to exist and people were either one of two categories: HIV symptomatic or asymptomatic.

There are additional problems. The predominant population being affected by the epidemic was gay men in urban areas. Increasingly, this has become less so. While the epidemic used to be viewed through a lens that showed having AIDS making people poor or homeless, it is well beyond the time to flip the lens and in fact see how AIDS is impacting the poor. Additionally, there are greater numbers of people being affected by AIDS who, had it not been for AIDS, would have no system of care at all. Consider, for example, the recidivism rate among prisoners in the State of California, which is 97 percent. Virtually all prisoners with HIV who leave California's prisons commit another crime so that they can return to the system of care they received while incarcerated because without it, they would have nothing. There is an increasing number of people—the chronically mentally ill, the chronically homeless, the chronically substance-addicted—who may never have had the benefit of any AIDS awareness whatsoever. There could be a hundred reasons. The reason is unimportant—the fact is that they exist and they are growing rapidly.

The result is that the safety net is more important than ever to them as they face the dual challenges of HIV and poverty. Yet, at the same time, this safety net is more vulnerable to fiscal pressures than ever before, and programs that support the disabled will, in all probability, become more difficult to access, with less available to you once you do gain entry. Nevertheless, the saftey net is a lifeline. Your experience may be frustrating and tiring, but as anyone will tell you, the key to making it less of a draining experience is to enter it prepared and organized.

When people with AIDS first began to apply for these benefit programs, they were often hampered by the fact that their diagnosis had been unexpected. This caused them to have to go back and piece everything together. Each time an agency or bureaucrat needed a form or a document signed, the person with AIDS had to go out and get it and bring it back. Today, many people are still diagnosed with HIV at the same time that they are diagnosed with AIDS, and that is unfortunate. But for people who have been tested and know their status, it is not an admission of getting sicker to prepare for the possibility that one day they may need these programs.

All of these complications posed a serious discouragement to people who genuinely needed to access the system. As seen in the last chapter, the need to get finances under control is an imperative since the alternative is irritating, time consuming, and undermining to a person's ability to focus on his or her own health and control over quality of life. And just as a person will feel that he is taking some control and authority back over his life from the virus by taking various forms of treatment such as antiretrovirals or holistic natural therapies, so does a person feel empowered when taking on the challenging benefits system and getting the results he needs. But in the early days, given the fear of social security workers and a bureaucracy that did not know how to treat a "new" disability, this seemed almost impossible.

In response, community-based organizations often set up benefits offices to assist applicants in getting the papers processed in a timely manner. In New York, the Gay Men's Health Crisis became in essence a social security office, processing papers there and sending them directly to an actual social security office to expedite the process. This procedure dealt with the situation of social security workers who were reluctant or unable to cope with people with AIDS. A decade later, the scene was much different, with Federal Emergency Management Agency (FEMA) representatives arriving at AIDS Project Los Angeles and the Los Angeles Gay and Lesbian Community Services Center (GLCSC) in 1994 to set up emergency stations in the wake of the Northridge earthquake, which devastated Los Angeles in January 1994. This marked the first time a federal agency ever came to an AIDS organization and a gay and lesbian organization to set up an outreach post. It took 10 years for the mountain to come to Mohammed. Today, of course, there are not the horrific problems connected to getting the benefits because of workers' fear of PWAs. Instead, the problems are connected to keeping the benefits one is entitled to.

These systems of support seem like a confusing maze, and not entirely without reason. The complications are there supposedly to serve as a check and balance against abuse of the system. Today, people are generally diagnosed with HIV disease at a much earlier level, allowing much greater quality of life during the period of time one knows one has HIV. However, in the 1980s, people had to cope with a great deal on top of the red tape to apply for and get their benefits.

The system, while complicated, is not as hostile or unaccomodating as it once was, if for no other reason than that the bureaucracy was able to respond to the new epidemic by including AIDS opportunistic infections as disabilities, thereby allowing people to gain benefits. In addition, the existence of an AIDS diagnosis now bestows upon an applicant "presumptive disability," meaning that the person applying for benefits is likely to be regarded by the system as disabled. In the early years of the epidemic, when T cell levels were an alien term and opportunistic infections, which had previously been unheard of, were becoming common, the system simply did not know how to respond. Today, the problem is not in getting the system to respond, but rather in understanding the system and getting through it. In the old days, access to the system was difficult because of an AIDS diagnosis; today access is difficult because the system is complicated whether or not your disability is due to AIDS.

HOW IT WORKS TODAY—APPLYING FOR BENEFITS

It is important to get caught by the safety net. To fall into it with the greatest of ease and avoid the potential of falling through a hole, there are steps you can take. The wealth of experience of people in the AIDS/HIV community over the past several years dictates this; the difference between a very bad experience or a not so bad experience in making your applications for assistance and entitlements is in one word—preparation. Making applications to entitlement programs is not impossible; it is somewhat hard but you can do it. It is like anything else outlined in this book. You can prepare and plan ahead, thereby substantially diminishing the potential for complications, or you can do nothing and let circumstances carry you where they will. By preparing, you are establishing that, as much as possible, you are the person in control of your destiny. *In not preparing yourself you run the risk of being beaten back by a big system and walking away with the label the press so often associates with people living with AIDS—a victim.* Therefore, plan ahead, take the steps to simplify your application process, and when you do, you will feel better about your circumstances. For the investment of time and effort now, you will save potential heartache later.

Things You Will Need Later, So Get Them Together Now

In the process of application for entitlement programs, you are going to need to provide a fair amount of information about your professional and your medical history. It is important to put some thought into this effort and put forth the facts as they occurred. If you are prepared ahead of time, it will save you time.

1. Find your birth certificate. A Xerox copy will get you nowhere. If you can't find your birth certificate, call the hospital where you were born and tell them you will need a certified copy; they will explain to you how to go about getting it. Or call the Hall of Records or City Hall where you were born.

2. Find your social security card. If you can't find it, you can write for a replacement. If for any reason you had more than one social security number, find the card for each one.

3. You will have to get your medical records to demonstrate your diagnosis of AIDS and the date that your disability began. Your application may be more complicated if you do not have an AIDS diagnosis or if you cannot demonstrate disability, even if you have fewer than 200 T cells. You will need to show that you are disabled from participating in gainful employment due to your HIV condition. This may slow up your application. Note that "gainful employment" is a term that refers to you doing a job—any job, not necessarily the one you were doing. This means that if you were a ballet dancer and you can no longer dance but could in fact be working in a bookstore full time, then you could be gainfully employed. Your medical condition must have prevented you from being gainfully employed for a period of at least 12 months.

4. If you have a résumé, look at it. The résumé should include a description of your past job duties. If there is no such description, update the résumé and include a narrative for each type of job you held during your work history.

5. Begin work on a second résumé. This time, it is your medical résumé. Go back in time and list each physician who attended to your medical care; record any hospitalizations, including the dates, where the hospital was, and the reason for your hospitalization; list your symptomol-

ogy; list your prescriptions. It is probably best to do this in chronological order. If you are someone who keeps a diary, it would be a good idea to go back and look at it in helping you complete your medical résumé.

6. As a taxpayer, you are supposed to keep your W-2 forms and your tax filings for several years. Ideally, you have done this. If you haven't, list the names and addresses of any employer who you have worked for during the past three years.

7. Any documentation of your financial status should be organized into a large file. Put together an accordion file that includes your bank statements, income tax returns, mortgage or rent agreement, documentation of your household expenditures, and the names of any persons who share the household with you. Include your car registration and car insurance policy if you own an automobile.

8. If you are married, you will need the social security numbers and possibly the birth dates of each person in the household, whether or not you have children.

You can get these materials together prior to anticipating a need to apply for benefits. Once you do decide to apply, you will be given an appointment to see a worker at the social security office. If you make your application for social security programs with these materials already in hand, your application path should be made smooth. In fact, if it is possible, obtain the application forms before any appointment you may get with a social security representative and fill them out, to the best of your ability, before you go to your appointment. If you go to apply without these materials, you will be asked to go back and get them. Delays can occur when a physician is late in delivering his or her records. Do it ahead of time.

It would be misleading to assume that because all of the above-referenced materials are gathered together and organized the application process is done. Being organized is only the starting point. The materials needed to accompany any application may involve the filing of several forms. By having the information with you, you will be able to file the forms with greater ease than if you get the materials together after sitting down with the forms. In some ways, it is like an open book test. You are able to look up the answers in the materials you bring with you, but you still have to fill out the test to pass the course.

Perhaps most important of all, find the copy machine that is nearest to you and most reliable and make copies of any materials connected with your application for benefits. Copy the materials you turn in as well as those turned in for you. If your physician sends anything in, have copies sent to you. If you send in anything, after copying it send it certified mail, return receipt requested.

To get detailed information on how to apply for federal entitlement programs in your area, call directory assistance. If you cannot find a social security office, telephone the AIDS service organization nearest you. If you do not know what that would be, telephone the Centers for Disease Control National Hotline number, 800-342-2437.

The length of time that an application takes will largely rely on where you make your application. Large urban areas tend to be slower due to the volume of cases they must process. Logic would dictate that a rural office might process the application faster, though there may be less familiarity with HIV issues that would slow up the process. Each state also may present factors that cause a variance in the application time.

THE FEDERAL PROGRAMS

Social Security Disability Income

This is a sort of "insurance policy" that most people who are working pay into through their employment. The eligibility for this program is based primarily on the fact that you are disabled. But to qualify for social security disability income (SSDI or sometimes SSD) you also must
- be unable to participate in gainful employment
- have been working for 20 out of the last 40 quarters and have paid into the system through your employer

- be a citizen or an alien who has received amnesty, though not for SSD
- have proof of disability as defined by SSA and documented by a physician[*]

Supplemental Security Income

This program is offered by the federal government to people who do not earn an amount that brings them up to a given level. Supplemental security income (SSI) will then add to that income. Therefore, in being able to take advantage of this program, you will need to meet its financial eligibility requirements, which will vary from state to state, given any contribution your state government may make to your income.

Medicaid

This is a government-sponsored health insurance plan for the poor that has eligibility requirements that are based on income. Medicaid has been a growing part of the federal budget and there have been many attempts to lower costs. Possibilities for the future almost certainly include Medicaid payments into systems of managed care or, in other words, health maintenance organizations (HMOs). It remains to be seen whether such a change would enhance medical care for the poor or merely cut government cost. Because the payments to providers of health care are inordinately low, private physicians who take Medicaid as a form of payment are very, very few, thereby restricting choice of physicians. Additional problems can arise if you are receiving a prescription for your condition that is not covered by Medicaid, though the system for

---

[*]It is extremely important to note that, upon your application for social security based on your disability, if you have a diagnosis of AIDS, you should have a presumptive disability status, allowing you to get six months of payments pending your application. However, having a T cell level that is under 200 in and of itself will not be sufficient to qualify, and disability will have to be demonstrated.

updating the list of drugs covered is much faster than it used to be. Not all hospitals willingly take a Medicaid patient either, and while such a patient will be admitted to an emergency room, he or she may be transferred to a facility that accepts Medicaid as a regular course of business, such as a public hospital. If you are a person who qualifies for supplemental security income, your eligibility for this program is extremely likely.

Medicare

This is a more advanced form of insurance than Medicaid and is extended to the elderly and to the disabled. The eligibility for this program is not based on income but rather on one's condition and the length of time disabled. All people qualify for Medicare at the age of 65. Thus, former president Ronald Reagan was able to use Medicare (and did) as are the poorest of the poor who may be disabled. As Medicare is not poverty based, it has distinct advantages over Medicaid, since it reimburses health-care providers at better rates and has a wider range of coverage. It is not as desirable as private insurance in most respects, but it is definitely advantageous to have. It is important for people with HIV to note that it is possible and in fact desirable to have both Medicaid and Medicare at the same time. One can achieve coverage under both programs after disability has lasted for 24 months of SSD benefits.

For people with HIV who have private insurance, it is also extremely important to take note of the fact that you should be able to maintain your private insurance through COBRA after leaving your employment (see Chapter 6). COBRA allows you to stay on a group plan through your employer, but you have to shoulder the burden of the costs of your share of the plan. Once your insurance period through COBRA runs out, if you were disabled from the time you entered into your COBRA insurance, you should be eligible for Medicare.

This means that your chronological insurance profile would be something like this:

- group insurance while working
- disabling HIV event occurs
- elect COBRA, stay on group plan, leave work on disability
- your participation in the group insurance ends
- Medicare coverage begins

Denial: Not Just a State of Mind

People familiar with HIV tend to think of denial as a state of mind, that time or state when one is apt to deny the reality of a situation because it is safer for the moment to do so. Denial can also be the cold harsh reality of an entitlement program saying that your application for benefits is being turned down.

If you have taken the steps outlined previously in making your application, your denial appeal will be easier. You have the right to appeal a denial for benefits.

There are four basic appeals available to anyone denied benefits from social security:

- reconsideration
- hearing by an administrative judge
- review by an appeals council
- federal court action

These appeals fall in this order.

At the first juncture of reconsideration, your application will be reviewed by new persons and any additional information you may add that may have been missing from your application or for which questions were raised by the original reviewer will enhance your chances of success.

If you are unsuccessful after a review, your case can be heard by an administrative law judge, a proceeding at which you may be present and at which you may present evidence of your disability.

Failing success at that level, you may request an appeal by an appeals council, which can decide the case itself or send it back down to the administrative law judge for reconsideration.

The least desirable action of all is the last appeal, which is the filing of a lawsuit against social security. This is not to imply that this route is not successful, but litigation in any form is time consuming and resource intensive. You should find legal representation to assist you.

THE STATE PROGRAMS

There may be various programs in your state that can also be of assistance. The only way to be sure of what is available is to find a resource in your area that can shape an overview for you of state programs. Again, your local AIDS service organization should be able to do this.

Some states will also supply direct funding to people with disabilities in addition to what may be available to you on the federal level, though the rules and programs will vary widely from state to state.

Short-Term Disability

There may be provision for the payment of short-term disability benefits, which would be based on a plan set up by the state government to insure employees in the event of disability.* The term is short and may cover you until such time as you are covered by long-term disability payments. You will, in all likelihood, only qualify for this benefit if you have paid into the system through your employer, a record of which is recorded on your pay stub.

Welfare

If health-care reform was the buzz topic for the 1992 presidential campaign, welfare reform shaped the 1996 debate. Welfare

---

*States that have such programs are California, New York, New Jersey, Rhode Island, and Hawaii.

programs are enormously different from state to state, supplying funding under a variety of eligibility criteria, restrictions, and lengths of time.

Food Stamps

Again, administered by states, whether or not you can be on social security and get food stamps will depend on the state in which you live. Food stamps are only available for the purchase of food and are not intended for anything that is a nonfood or luxury item such as tobacco or alcohol.

Insurance Premium Payments

It makes sense for a state to supply insurance premiums subsidies to persons with disabilities who might lose their insurance if they can no longer afford the premiums. For the investment, the state keeps the person from entering the rolls of the state administered and partially funded Medicaid program, thereby saving money. Nevertheless, not every state has such a program available.

CONCLUSION

In the coming years, the resources available to people under these programs, either state or federal, are going to be diminished in the interest of balancing the budgets of our governmental jurisdictions. Eligibility requirements and standards are going to get tougher. It is therefore more instrumental than ever that you be prepared to be your own advocate or have a friend or social worker help you, being as organized and prepared as possible for all of the documentation and information you will need to supply in order to get caught by the safety net.

Steps and Resources

- *Step*—locate as many of the materials as possible named above
- *Step*—find someone who has been through this already and get their advice
- *Step*—keep a medical journal
- *Resource*—local social security office
- *Resource*—hospital social work department
- *Resource*—your AIDS service organization

5

On the Job
A History of Discrimination

Prejudice: A vagrant opinion
without visible means of support.

Ambrose Bierce
The Devil's Dictionary

Discrimination is nothing new. It has always been and probably will always be. As it pertains to people with HIV, discrimination is only one more obstacle, one more challenge.

The foundation for acts of discrimination is the separation of one person, or one kind of person, from others, treating that person differently because of a particular distinctive characteristic or set of characteristics that vary from the norm. This is a complicated way to say that discrimination is often an expression of mob rule.

There are many who might argue that freedom from discrimination was forfeited by people with HIV by culpable behavior that resulted in their getting AIDS in the first place, such as sex or drugs. Discrimination, however, not only clashes with our democratic ideals, it also undermines the greater public good when it affects the way we administer to our own public health. AIDS/HIV discrimination gets in the way of the public good *and* violates our notions of equality.

81

BACKGROUND—WHAT IS DISCRIMINATION?

"It is ironic," explains David Schulman, head of the Los Angeles City Attorney AIDS/HIV Discrimination Unit, "that, in part, my sensitivity about discrimination and AIDS discrimination in particular comes from an unlikely source." Schulman explains that his grandparents were European Jewish immigrants who came to the United States, traveling not just a long way in distance, but in many respects, in time. "In terms of culture," he says, "they had to travel such a tremendous journey—from nineteenth century Europe to, eventually, mid-twentieth century southern California. That journey gave me a perspective about change and tolerance that has had an important effect on my work."

Schulman himself grew up in Long Beach, California, where he found himself to be the token ethnic growing up in his neighborhood: "This caused me to lead two parallel lives. The first one was where I behaved like a good WASP, playing Little League, joining the Cub Scouts, and even going to YMCA camp one summer. I managed to ignore people's comments about my curly hair." Parallel to that, he explains, he led a rich life within the context of the Jewish community of Long Beach.

"And I think that sense of both belonging and passing—and not passing and not trying to pass—had a lot to do with my own responsiveness to other people who have faced similar questions about identity, as with people who are gay or lesbian."

What Schulman describes is a life affected by discrimination. Even within his own identity, he made attempts to live as both Gentile and Jew, much as gay and lesbian people often have to exist in a world that is both gay and straight. Each day, each of us chooses to carry out hundreds of acts of discrimination, while at the same time we are each victim of one kind of discrimination or another. Discrimination is inherent in our everyday decision making. Each day, we choose chocolate over vanilla, this shirt over that shirt. We discriminate hundreds of times a day. Hence, most forms of discrimination are actually legal, but others, which may put people on an unfair playing field, damaging their dignity as individuals or as a class of individuals and violating a norm of equality and fairness, are not legal. Historically, certain groups have been treated unfairly and the law has sought to redress that treatment because discrimination in specific settings is simply incongruous with our concepts of liberty and democracy. That incongruity may appear more obvious to some judges and lawmakers in the cases of race and gender than it does with sexual orientation and disability.

The supreme law of the land, the Constitution of the United States, bans certain types of discrimination from occurring. Who is protected from discrimination? The law scrutinizes certain types of discriminatory acts more closely than others. If an act of discrimination is committed against a person who is in a category of race, ethnicity, religion, or gender, the standard of the law is rigorous and demanding in reacting to discrimination because the law is scrutinizing and jealous of rights due those persons. However, lesbian and gay persons are viewed by the law and the courts as classes who, while they deserve some protection, are not historically entitled to heightened protection. Consequently, the law is less rigorous because the rights of these classes of people are not as clearly enunciated. Thus, even the legal system discriminates.

Beyond the "who" in discrimination law, there is the "what." Discrimination in certain private settings is often deemed to be out of the jurisdiction of discrimination safeguards, which therefore do not give a person a cause of action or reason to sue. For the most part, however, people with AIDS early in the epidemic suffered heavily from the kinds of discrimination that most people will never have to face and that now give reason to sue, but only after hard-fought legal battles paved the way.

A Natural History of AIDS Discrimination

In the early 1980s, gay men in urban America were the population most affected by AIDS. The World Health Organization reports that there were 189 cases of AIDS in the United States in 1981 and that 75 percent of those cases were either in New York or California, with 97 percent of them among men. (By contrast, in

1990, there were 43,000 new cases reported, throughout every state in the nation, 11 percent of which were women and 800 of which were children.) Following gay men were injection drug users and Haitians, who were classified by the medical establishment and by the media as "risk groups." Nationally, the most visible of these groups was and still is gay men, as today they comprise 60 percent of the AIDS diagnoses occurring. In the decades before there was such a thing as AIDS, the push for equal rights for gay men and lesbians had seen modest progress, beginning most significantly with the 1969 Stonewall riot in Greenwich Village in New York. From that point, the profile of gays in society became less closeted. The gay and lesbian movement was also carried along and buoyed by the sexual revolution that began in the 1960s, though for many gays, even then the closet door would remain shut. Sex lives and professional lives remained distinctly separate.

Eventually, however, the AIDS epidemic pulled that closet door open, causing a person to reveal for the first time to an employer and perhaps a family that not only was he or she gay, but in addition had a fatal and frightening disease. This disease killed quickly, and in 1981 it didn't even have a proper name. First called GRID, for Gay Related Immune Deficiency, it later became AIDS—Acquired Immune Deficiency Syndrome. The reaction of families was often more severe to the news that a son or brother was dying because he had had sex with another man than it was to the fact that he was dying. In the perception of the public, AIDS was a problem that did not belong to society, but to an "other" within society. It was not a problem considered by mainstream society to be "our" problem; it was "their" problem. This attitude marginalized AIDS, putting distance between the public and the disease.

Even among gay men, there was a desire to keep the epidemic away. When AIDS was called GRID, the theory was generally put forth that the disease resulted in the destruction of the immune system because of a lifestyle accompanied by a stream of sexually transmitted diseases. Their subsequent antibiotic treatment, along with late nights, drug abuse, and, in general, high living was thought to have a synergistic effect that depleted the immune system. Gay men who were sexually conservative felt secure, then, in believing that AIDS was not their problem.

Blaming the disease on lifestyle found a comfortable niche in the psyche of almost everyone and continues well into the epidemic, with Senator Jesse Helms blaming gays for their illness as recently as 1995. Pigeonholing AIDS in this manner sent two potent messages: (1) if you do not lead this lifestyle, you are safe from this disease, and (2) "they" got what "they" deserve, an attitude historically popular during epidemics. The lifestyle theory, in turn, allowed gay men who didn't have such a lifestyle to feel safe and insulated from the epidemic. Heterosexuals and women, feeling that it was only a gay problem, felt even safer. Everyone, in short, sought to compartmentalize the epidemic. This desire was borne from an overwhelming desire to believe oneself to be safe from the effects of the epidemic, keeping it in one or another sector of our society.

The earliest incidents of AIDS discrimination, it should be remembered, occurred before the development of the HIV-antibody test, which was not licensed until 1985. From 1982 to 1985, the most likely scenario for discrimination occurred when a gay man was noticed to have lost weight or developed a persistent cough, presenting the possibility that he had anything from the flu to AIDS. While discrimination is typically thought of in terms of employment, it occurs on every level, in formal relationships, such as those with employers, landlords, providers of service, but also in informal relationships with friends and family. Discrimination can be overt or covert, and while some relationships can and are governed by law, most, in fact, are not. In its earliest forms, AIDS discrimination was rampant in both formal and informal relationships and was almost always overt rather than covert. A gay man in New York or San Francisco with a limp wrist and persistent cough could find himself fired and estranged from family and friends in a very short time. But there have been as many kinds of discrimination as one can imagine. As late as 1993, the Yokohama Chamber of Commerce discovered in a survey that one-third of all companies doing business in Japan believed that HIV-positive employees should be isolated from others in some fashion. Health-care professionals have grown reluctant to administer mouth-to-mouth resuscitation for fear of contracting AIDS. Health insurance companies cap the amount of money that will be paid for AIDS, even though they may not do so for cancer or other expensive illnesses.

AIDS discrimination has also evolved over time in its nature, speed, and subtlety. In the earliest days of AIDS, people with AIDS did not live very long. In the later years of the epidemic, with greater numbers of people being tested for HIV antibodies, more people became aware of their HIV-antibody status at an early stage of infection. In 1985, for example, there were 79,000 HIV-antibody tests performed in the United States. Only five years later, in 1991, there were 2,091,000 tests performed. But prior to the development of the test, people generally discovered that they had HIV at the same time they found out they had AIDS—when they were presenting symptoms of pneumocystis pneumonia (PCP) at an emergency room or when, one day, a purple spot appeared on an ankle, a torso, or a forearm, and a biopsy revealed Kaposi's Sarcoma. These two scenarios were very different settings for discrimination. The early days were marked with a quick reaction to an AIDS diagnosis while discrimination later took on a subtle form, and reactions were not only to people who had the disease but also to people suspected of having it. After 1985, a positive HIV test provided more than mere medical information; it became a marker for discrimination.

Discrimination did not occur merely between individuals; whole institutions became deeply involved. Healthcare facilities, certainly insurance companies, and even government bureaucracies such as social security offices discriminated against people with AIDS in the most obvious ways, as illustrated throughout this book. Insurance companies, wanting to cut the possibility of severe financial losses, would "redline" certain neighborhoods that were predominantly homosexual, such as West Hollywood, California, or Greenwich Village, New York. Moreover, companies would refuse group insurance to businesses considered to be densely populated with gays, such as florists, gay bars, restaurants, design firms, and, later, doctors' offices where high numbers of people with HIV were treated.

These types of discrimination prompted the active development of early AIDS community-based organizations such as the Gay Men's Health Crisis, the first AIDS service organization in the fight against AIDS, the San Francisco AIDS Foundation, and AIDS Project Los Angeles, to name a few. These were organizations made up of people concerned about AIDS, who came together and took care of themselves when no one else was going to do it. AIDS service organizations in many ways symbolize early AIDS discrimination, when whole systems were engaged in discrimination against people with AIDS. The gay community reacted by starting its own organizations, replacing ineffective or unwilling mainstream systems, or by mounting effective advocacy to challenge discrimination practiced by mainstream systems. In effect, the development of today's large AIDS service organizations may be attributable to the ugly specter of AIDS discrimination.

In addition, the gay and lesbian community began to mount legal services and responses to the issues being faced by people with HIV. The Lambda Legal Defense Fund began early work in landmark court cases concerning AIDS discrimination.

Government slowly began to respond to discrimination. The response, though slow in coming, was one urged by public health officials and lawyers alike. It began at the local level and crept upward toward an AIDS-silent president. The public health strategy to fight the epidemic was based on creating an atmosphere that would encourage people to come forward voluntarily to be tested for HIV antibodies, to learn their HIV status, and to begin taking AZT (or, now, other antiretrovirals such as DDI). As a result of learning their status, they would, it was hoped, refrain from activities, either drug-related or sexual, that would cause the spread of AIDS. Mandatory testing proposals, it was argued, simply would be too expensive to be effective in catching HIV, not to mention legally problematic.

Courts responded by recognizing that existing laws that prohibited discrimination against persons with a handicap or disability protected the rights of people with AIDS. Local and state
governments responded by passing legislation that was HIV-specific or that expanded existing disability protections to include
people with HIV or discrimination against persons with AIDS,
thereby supporting public health and attempting to make the
environment safer for testing and treatment.

Why Do People Discriminate?

The causes of discrimination are many and run deep. Acts of
discrimination cannot be attributable to simple ignorance or malice. Just as HIV is medically complex, AIDS itself presents a complex sociological web of fearful elements that are known to cause
fear, combining the long-standing societal taboos about sex, death,
and drugs. Fear of any one of these taboos is substantial, but in
combination they become a particularly powerful setting for discrimination. In particular, fear of mortality cannot be underplayed
in light of the ways in which our society has sought to distance itself
from issues of death and dying. David Schulman believes, in fact,
that western society's fear of death and dying is more pronounced
than ever, observing that in this century we have removed ourselves as far as possible from both birth and death:

"Modern living has isolated most Americans from the daily
presence of death in a way that has been unprecedented in human
culture. With slaughterhouses in one place, and hospitals in another place, most Americans live their daily lives without the
presence of death."

Schulman notes the ways in which modern culture has, by its
very nature, pushed itself away from experiences of death and
dying: "Grandparents don't die in the bedroom surrounded by the
extended family, and chickens aren't plucked and butchered before
we eat them." He notes researchers who have observed that "the
lack of familiarity with death in our culture has layered additional
phobic qualities on to the terror people have always had about

death and dying." In short, events that might have provoked one to ponder death and our relationship to it have, for the most part, been removed from our daily life, making it more a mystery, more something that one may fear.

"We don't even have a word for this kind of fear about death and dying in our language," says Schulman. A person with AIDS, he concludes, symbolizes everything we have tried to get away from in the twentieth century. "A person with AIDS points up our own vulnerability at a time when we thought we were invulnerable. A person with AIDS, perhaps most of all, is a constant reminder that our belief that science can cure everything, from water pollution to global warming, is a fallacy and that while we immunized ourselves against many diseases with the advances of modern science, we now know that we are at risk." Perhaps adding insult to injury, a disease like AIDS points up the fact that as powerful as we believe we may be as individuals, the existence of a single type of cell in our bloodstreams can suddenly and harshly take control over our lives. AIDS says to each individual, "You are not as powerful as you thought you were." AIDS is a great equalizer, and that makes people uncomfortable and afraid. It is this fear that may motivate people more than any other. This fear, says Schulman, is greatly overlooked as a reason people discriminate against people with AIDS.

The lynchpin for an act of discrimination is stigma, something that sets one apart from others, causing one for many reasons to become a scapegoat, a focal point for anger and scorn that are largely symbolic. The stigma, in fact, acts as the lightning rod and can take on a variety of forms. David Schulman found it in his own background: "Those descended from European Jews who have any sense of history know that their forebears often functioned in the role of scapegoat for European society. And that concept of scapegoat is intimately related to stigma and pollution. If you dress and worship differently, that can easily be defined by the group in power as not merely being different, but as stigmatizing."

Thus, if you have the stigma of HIV infection or of being gay or a drug user, then you become the object of many powerful fears about sex, drugs, and most of all, dying. This stigma is so powerful that it has colored the entire way public health has approached AIDS, treating it differently from other epidemics.

"This is a plague," says Schulman, "and historically, people respond to plagues badly because they disrupt the social order and point up society's vulnerability. And in late twentieth century America, AIDS challenges society's belief that science had made us invulnerable to new epidemics."

The reason for society's poor response is simple—it is because of fear. This fear can have two effects: one that motivates rational behavior and another that motivates irrational behavior. It is important to emphasize that it is not the fear itself that is irrational; everyone's fear needs to be respected because it is real. There is very good reason for a person to fear AIDS because AIDS kills people.

But the ways in which people may react out of fear do not necessarily merit respect. The classic example of a fire in a crowded movie theater illustrates the point. If there is a fire, it is a rational thing for people to be afraid. The fire will kill you. Your fear of the fire will stimulate a response. Your response, on the one hand, might be to shout and push and clamor to get out of the theater, thereby causing panic, a possible stampede resulting in people becoming needlessly hurt or even killed. As a result of the panic, people may be put at even greater risk than if they were facing only the fire. On the other hand, if the fear stimulates a response that is organized and orchestrated and subdues panic, the chances are greatly improved that everyone who can be saved will be saved.

The law, in an effort to support public health and to respect people's fears, had to find a balance when it came to its response to AIDS discrimination. If an environment of panic prevailed, people would be needlessly hurt and even killed. If a public health strategy to get people tested through voluntary means was to be successful, an orderly and calm response by the law was needed. While people's fear merited respect, irrational behavior could not go unchallenged. To do otherwise would have fanned the flames of an epidemic already out of control.

The First AIDS Discrimination Cases

"I feel as if I am trying to empty the ocean with a spoon," wrote David Schulman in his journal in 1986. He was new to his job as the head of the AIDS discrimination unit in the Los Angeles City Attorney's office. People were afraid; they didn't know how to act around people with AIDS. There were growing numbers of acts of discrimination committed against all kinds of people with AIDS everywhere in the United States.

The City of Los Angeles responded with the passage of the nation's first HIV-specific antidiscrimination law in 1985. The ordinance was passed because of elected officials' alarm at the experiences of Los Angelenos against whom people had begun to discriminate. In an environment where people were only introduced to AIDS for the first time by the diagnosis of Rock Hudson, there was little knowledge about AIDS and few resources available for getting knowledge.

"There was a great amount of public concern and anxiety about the meaning of the city's new AIDS antidiscrimination law," says Schulman. "It was difficult for people to accept that our law required folks to let infected people be out among them."

There were other problems as well. People found that their leases could not be renewed or they could not move into apartments. Their doctors told them to leave the office and not return. Their dentists refused flat out to see them. Schools refused to admit them. They were refused entry onto buses. The social security office would not process their forms. The nurse would not bring the tray of food into the hospital room. Sheets were left unchanged. Family members refused people with AIDS entry to a reunion. Nephews and nieces were kept away by brothers and sisters. Lovers left.

"In the early years," says Schulman, "the majority of our cases were employment related. There were employers who were bewildered as to what their duties were and who were also frightened themselves, who were perhaps somewhat homophobic, and who didn't know what to do with a sick employee." Basically, in the early years of the epidemic, a person's entire support system, both institutional and personal, evaporated more quickly than his or her immune system.

It is difficult to distinguish the motivations of individuals in these circumstances. Some react out of fear, some react out of judgment. In the eyes of the law, it doesn't matter.

The law as it preexisted AIDS forbade discrimination against persons with a disability or handicap in the primary settings:

- in places of employment
- in places of public accommodation
- in housing

In other words, an employer could not discharge an employee for developing a handicap, nor could people be barred from eating in restaurants or renting an apartment.

Handicap discrimination laws had already appeared in most states at the time the AIDS epidemic began, though not all states had them (such as Arizona and Delaware). These laws made it illegal to discriminate against a person with a handicap and offered varying degrees of protection. Some local laws also existed with the same purpose, especially in large metropolitan areas. Federally, there was the Vocational Rehabilitation Act of 1973, which also made it illegal to discriminate against persons with a handicap.

Thus, there was already a law protecting people with disabilities from discrimination, and HIV-specific protections were also passed. This meant that a person who was discriminated against had several places to look for laws that offered remedy. First, there may be law at the local level, either city or county. Second, there may be a state statute. Lastly, there is federal law. Which remedy you seek may depend on where the strongest laws are, what the easiest way is to get to them, and whether or not there is jurisdiction of the laws over your case. "Jurisdiction" refers to which administrative government is the lawmaker: local, state, or federal. A local government passes laws that affect people only locally. A city cannot pass a law telling a state or federal government what it must do. Therefore, even if New York City has a law prohibiting discrimination, if you live outside of New York City you must look for a state law to protect you. Jurisdiction, however, may also be determined by whom you work for. For example, if a state and a city both have laws prohibiting discrimination but you are a federal employee, neither the city nor the state has the power to tell the federal government what to do. Therefore, a federal employee who wants to bring an antidiscrimination action must rely on federal law.

Here is an example of jurisdictional complications: Let's say that John Doe lives in Arizona, where his employer has seen that he has become handicapped and has fired him. John Doe finds that there are no local statutes to protect him and no state statutes, but he knows that there is the Federal Rehabilitation Act offering antidiscrimination protection to persons with a handicap. Can he use it?

Even though John Doe is not a federal employee, he may still be able to use the Federal Rehabilitation Act if his employer received federal funding for some purpose. In that event, getting federal funds is a nexus to the federal government, and he could use federal law. Of course, if John Doe works for the federal government, then he can definitely use federal law. But if his employer is a private employer entirely and does not receive federal dollars for any activity, then John Doe's ability to use federal law for handicap protection is nonexistent in a state without its own protections. Prior to the passage of the Americans with Disabilities Act (ADA) in 1990, he would have been without legal remedy. However, the ADA changed the horizon considerably, making it illegal for an employer with fifteen or more employees to discriminate against an employee on the basis of AIDS or HIV.

If, however, John Doe worked in New York City, then he would be able to choose for himself among city laws or state laws and even federal laws, if his employer had a federal nexus of some kind or if he were a federal employee. In that case, his choice of which law he would use to seek protection might be guided solely by issues of speed and access.

There was a problem with the early cases brought under handicap statutes. There was uncertainty as to whether or not AIDS was a handicap (or disability) for any of the laws that prohibited discrimination against a person with a handicap (or disability). When lawyers and judges go to trial over an issue, they look to three areas in which to make arguments and decision. In order of priority they are

- *Law*—existing laws and statutes specific to the topic at hand
- *Precedent*—decisions in similar cases set down by courts before them
- *Written authority*—articles published in law reviews, presenting researched topics of law and making an argument for one or another position

When the first AIDS discrimination cases were brought to court, they were brought under the theory that AIDS was a handicap and that it was illegal to discriminate against a person with a handicap. The other side would argue that AIDS was not a handicap, it was a communicable disease.

Accordingly, courts first looked to law. There was no AIDS law because AIDS was a new situation. There were only the original laws prohibiting discrimination against a person who was handicapped or disabled. They then looked to precedent to see what courts before them had decided, and again there was none. They then looked to authority and there found a handful of law review articles that had researched the issue of whether or not a communicable disease like AIDS could be considered a handicap or disability and they concluded that it should be. That is how the early cases were won.

These early cases involved people who had been diagnosed with what was called "full-blown" AIDS. On the strength that AIDS was a handicap and that it was illegal to discriminate against persons with a handicap, the early cases were won.

During the years 1982 to 1985, it first appeared that such victories might lead to a lower level of discrimination. A second large wave of cases began to occur among people who did not have "full-blown" AIDS but rather were either known to be infected with HIV, or, because of a limp wrist or other affectation, were thought to be at risk and therefore likely to be carrying the virus—people perceived to have HIV.

During 1985 and 1986, three events occurred that are still three of the most profound events in HIV/AIDS history: the virus (then called HTLV-III) was isolated; a subsequent antibody test was developed; and actor Rock Hudson was diagnosed. These three events, two a scientific advance and one a social footnote, caused an enormous reaction and had a historic effect on AIDS discrimination.

The diagnosis of Rock Hudson, then starring in *Dynasty*, a popular television nighttime soap opera, put a face on AIDS. In the minds of many Americans, if asked when AIDS began, they would say that it was in 1985 with the actor's revelation. AIDS jumped from the background of everyone's mind to the foreground, with little or no accompanying education about the disease. Still relatively little was known about the disease and when transmission factors were enunciated by scientists and by the government, people tended to disbelieve them. AIDS raised many more questions than there were answers.

Little about AIDS could be expressed in black or white answers. Yes, one could say with absolute certainty that AIDS was not casually spread by hugging or by toilet seats. But other responses were often gray, relative in their explanation, offering less reassurance, and difficult for the public to grasp. After the four previous years of near silence about AIDS, radio and television talk and call-in shows were suddenly crowding the air waves with AIDS stories. And wherever there was little or no knowledge, there was a breeding ground for discrimination.

"Can you say with 100 percent certainty that my child won't contract AIDS in the schoolyard?" people wanted to know.

"Can you say with 100 percent certainty that I won't get AIDS from my doctor?"

"No," said scientists and doctors, *"nothing is 100 percent certain, but it is not probable."*

No physician or scientist would go before the public to swear that any concoction of events or circumstances couldn't lead to

AIDS transmission. But the truth was, no doctor could say with 100 percent certainty that a child wouldn't be killed on the playground by men from Mars. Anything is scientifically conceivable. Everything is of relative risk.

The development of the HIV test, on the other hand, occurring roughly at the same time, gave science the first significant tool with which to begin to fight the epidemic, yet also made available a tool for discrimination. The new test, combined with a climate of fear and little available information to change it, expanded the circle of discrimination.

In 1985, with heightened awareness about AIDS but low levels of actual knowledge about it, it was no longer only gay white men who had been diagnosed who experienced discrimination at the hands of employers, schools, places of public accommodation, and landlords, but people who, for one reason or another, might be perceived to have AIDS. The HIV antibody test became available not only as a blood screening tool but as a means of discrimination. As the years went by, the circle of discrimination widened to encompass all those affected by AIDS, from gays to Haitians to drug users to poor women of color to doctors who treated people with AIDS.

A Turning Point for AIDS Protections

Motivation for legislative bodies to do something about discrimination was not solely based on compassionate humanitarian concerns, but, as earlier stated, on the fear that discrimination threatened to undermine public health in very important ways. Caught between the growing political pressure brought to bear by AIDS organizations and activists and pressures to support public health strategy in the face of the epidemic, elected officials became motivated to act. In fact, perhaps frightened by the alarmingly increasing numbers of caseloads and the mystique of the disease, legislators began to enact antidiscrimination laws and confidentiality laws (see Chapter 8), relying on the expertise of public health officials.

When the circle of discrimination widened to include people perceived to have AIDS, the existing handicaps statutes often had to be stretched by the courts. In New York, state law covered people with handicaps as well as those *perceived* to have a handicap for one reason or another.

One woman in New York in 1986, whose fiancé died of AIDS, missed several days from work immediately after he died. When she returned to work, she confided to a friend what had happened. The following day, an armed security guard came to her desk and escorted her from the premises. She was told she was not to return unless she could produce an HIV antibody test that was negative. She did not want to take the HIV test at that time, and if she did take it, she did not wish to disclose the results to her employer. She began an administrative action with the state.

The normal remedy for a discrimination action where the issue is termination from employment is reinstatement to the position with back pay. In truth, she did not want her job back because she felt that her employer had acted reprehensibly. However, she did want her paycheck and her health insurance. The matter was settled before a formal determination in the matter, as most of the cases were. However, it bears noting that this woman became a target for discrimination because of two things: she was perceived to have AIDS because of her association with a person who was infected, and there was a test for HIV antibodies. She was a black Hispanic woman, and both African Americans and Hispanics living in the Bronx were increasingly considered a "high risk group."

In another case, in Westchester County, New York, two school-children were dismissed from school, not because they had AIDS, not because one of their parents had AIDS, but because an uncle, who did not live with the family, did have AIDS. The two children, by virtue of their association with someone with AIDS, became victims of discrimination. Again, they were protected under New York law because they were perceived to have a handicap. Schools are places of public accommodation. Antidiscrimination statutes usually protect people from discrimination in settings of employment, housing, and public accommodation.

Says David Schulman, "Virtually all AIDS discrimination in my experience comes from someone learning someone else's status who's not equipped to understand the meaning of the status." Even with the compassionate, he says, "The weight of that information starts to distort people's behavior. I'm thinking of the employee who tells her best friend at work, and the best friend is a great friend on Day One, but by Day Three says—'Oh, I'm not sure what I should do, I think maybe I need to tell my supervisor . . . ' and that is when the problems begin."

Both California and New York were jurisdictions that had state handicap protections, and Los Angeles had an HIV-specific statute. However, a federal employee in New York, such as a postal worker, or an employee in Delaware, where there were no handicap protections, would have to rely on federal law. The Federal Rehabilitation Act was the statute offering protection, and a person seeking remedy would have to go through the Equal Employment Opportunity Commission (EEOC).

There was a great deal of controversy about whether or not the act would cover AIDS as a disability. Despite widespread acceptance of AIDS as a handicap or disability among states with disability laws, the federal law had been untested.

In 1986, the Reagan administration, through Attorney General Edwin Meese, issued a Justice Department memorandum that made the front pages of major newspapers across America. In it, the attorney general's office effectively stated that AIDS discrimination might be technically illegal under the act; however, if there could be a showing that the workplace was impacted by a genuine fear of contagion among co-workers of the infected person, then discharge of the HIV-infected person might be appropriate. This memorandum was, in effect, a blueprint for how to carry out an act of discrimination.

About that same time, a woman named Jean Arline who lived and taught school in Florida, was discovered to have tuberculosis. As a teacher in public school, her school received federal funding and therefore was within the jurisdiction of the act. Tuberculosis, like HIV, is a communicable disease. She was discharged from her job because of her condition, and she began an action claiming discrimination under the act. Her case made it all the way to the

United States Supreme Court by 1987, several months after the justice department memorandum.

Her case won the attention of people all around the United States. In cases at the Supreme Court, the court accepts *amicus curae* briefs, which are briefs from "friends of the court." In this case, they received many such briefs. Senators, congressmen, legal defenders, and special interest groups from all over the United States submitted *amicus* briefs. However, very few of these briefs discussed the issue of TB as a handicap for purposes of the act. Rather, many or most discussed the issue of AIDS. Of primary interest to people concerned about HIV was the question of whether or not a communicable disease could be recognized as a handicap for purposes of the federal law.

The Supreme Court issued a seven to two decision, which was very decisive for that court, stating that the Federal Rehabilitation Act, which prohibited discrimination against a person with a handicap, did in fact consider TB, a communicable disease, to be a handicap. The court declined to discuss the issue of AIDS because Ms. Arline did not have HIV. Nevertheless, the case was still a landmark one for HIV legal defenders, standing for the very important principle that a communicable disease could be a handicap, thereby closing that loophole to opponents of discrimination protection. If they wanted to claim AIDS/HIV could not be covered under the act, they would have to find another way. The Arline decision was a major victory.

After the Arline decision came down from the Supreme Court, the U.S. Justice Department, no longer under Attorney General Edwin Meese, changed its mind and issued a new memorandum stating that AIDS discrimination, upon further reflection, was illegal for purposes of the Federal Rehabilitation Act.

FIGHTING AIDS DISCRIMINATION TODAY

Even with the Arline decision and the turnaround of the Justice Department, the issue of AIDS as a handicap remained somewhat unresolved because federal law only covered those employers who would receive federal funding of some kind, but all other employers were free to discriminate. However, during the Bush administration, a bill was proposed and passed in 1990 called the Americans with Disabilities Act (ADA). The ADA emphasizes the rights of disabled Americans to equal treatment on the job and in places of accommodation, such as city buses. It requires an employer to make a reasonable accommodation for disabled employees and bars discrimination against such persons.

Apart from its importance as landmark legislation for all disabled Americans, this legislation marked the first time that HIV was addressed in any federal statute. The ADA bars discrimination against persons with a handicap or disability and specifically outlines what constitutes a disability. The ADA applies to employers, landlords, and places of public accommodation. It is also important to note that the ADA specifically states what is not a disability.*

The ADA provides a remedy to discrimination by providing for damages as well as the restoration of one's job with back pay. However, when the complaint is one of public accommodation, the ability to gain a remedy may vary. This is so because the public accommodation provisions of the ADA are within the U.S. Justice Department. Therefore, enforcement or use of the ADA may be affected by political winds of the time. In addition, the offices of the U.S. Attorney General are charged with a broad range of civil rights enforcement and their capacity may vary from office to office. It is not necessary for one to utilize the U.S. Attorney General's office to bring suit under the ADA, but hiring a private attorney may require that a plaintiff supply money up front, which may present a barrier. In short, like any litigation, it can be time consuming and expensive.

---

*During the passage of the act, some conservative senators joined forces to amend the ADA to state that a disability shall not be considered to include homosexuality, bisexuality, pedophelia, tranvestism, transexualism, pyromania, or beastiality.

Bringing an AIDS Discrimination Case

Obviously, the conditions that surround lawsuits in HIV discrimination have changed greatly. The beginning of the epidemic saw very little in AIDS-specific legislation, particularly on a federal level, and one had to rely on statutes that were not HIV specific. The outcome was a little more uncertain. Today, many jurisdictions, including the federal government, talk specifically about HIV discrimination.

But the way discrimination occurs has also changed, becoming more subtle. As noted, in the beginning of the epidemic people did not know their sero status because there was no HIV-antibody test. This meant that they were involved in a discrimination case when they were very, very sick, and discrimination occurred usually at the point when they showed symptoms of AIDS. Today, with the advent of HIV-antibody testing and the early intervention of antiretrovirals into the course of the disease, the typical HIV discrimination client is much healthier and the discrimination is less blatant.

Employers are now more sophisticated about HIV, and consequently the nature of AIDS discrimination has changed greatly. With greater HIV knowledge, there are lower levels of fear. However, sometimes more practical elements of motivation come into play when it comes to discrimination. (The term "practical" in this context is meant only to imply that the discrimination is less based in emotion and more in calculated thought, not that it is in any way fair or reasonable.) An employer, for instance, may be less inclined to fire someone out of fear of contagion. Rather, his motive may rest in the fact that the costs of maintaining a person with AIDS will impact the company's insurance premiums, causing them to increase since he has a person with a disability on his payroll.

Therefore, David Schulman recommends that a person who is considering bringing a suit prepare for the case in the same way any other client in any other case must prepare: "Witnesses, documentation, notes, and preferably a pattern of bad acts rather than a single instance. That is a recipe that describes why so many AIDS discrimination cases are difficult to win." Each of these components is important in making your case. The more subtle the discrimination, or the conditions that cause the discrimination, the more you will need to record and document in order to show a pattern of behavior that reflects discrimination. When people were fired from their jobs with employers making statements to the effect that "Gee, your AIDS condition makes it so that we can't keep you on," such a pattern wasn't really necessary. But today, discrimination can be shown through a series of reassignments to less desirable jobs or making conditions of employment generally undesirable to you so that you will leave on your own accord (for example, see Chapter 7).

"It is the same reason," says Schulman, "that so many other discrimination cases can be difficult, and in that sense, are more difficult today with second generation cases than in the early days. Then an employer would send someone home, afraid to catch AIDS from a computer terminal," In today's environment, an employer clearly knows to say that an employee was discharged because of poor performance, not because of an AIDS condition. This assertion is a much more involved and difficult position to take on for a client bringing a case.

It means, however, that as obvious as the acts of discrimination may appear to you, you want as much documentation as possible. Copies of all your performance reviews, a schedule of all merit increases in pay or bonuses, character references, diary entries both personal and medical, and doctor reports may all be important in making the difference in your case. It will not be easy and may, in fact, prove very difficult. However, it is not impossible, and people with little documentation of their case should not be discouraged from talking to a lawyer. Documentation is important but need not be everything.

With respect to what form of discrimination one may encounter, this too has changed with the evolving landscape of AIDS. Schulman looks at the cases that have come through the city attorney's office in Los Angeles and sees that the early cases were employment related or involved people ignorant of the basics of AIDS. "I haven't had a landlord–tenant case where the apartment manager is afraid of letting the tenant use the pool or laundry facilities in years." Still, he says, "that doesn't mean I might not get another one, but for me that is typical of the 1980s, not the 1990s."

In more recent years there has been an increase in cases involving doctors' and dentists' refusal to treat, a practice that is banned by the Americans with Disabilities Act (see Chapter 9), as well as a burgeoning number of cases involving benefits, particularly private benefits but also public benefits (see Chapter 4). "Now," says Schulman, "more people learn that they are positive, but are otherwise healthy enough to work, but find that they experience some kind of benefits discrimination."

"Benefits" can mean those that are private, as with insurance, or public, as in the case of entitlement programs such as social security. Perhaps one of the most notorious types of discrimination seen with benefits is what is called "capping," or the practice by private insurance companies of limiting the amounts of money payable in response to claims on an insurance policy that are AIDS-related. (For more on capping, see Chapter 6.)

Where Discrimination Is Covered by Law

As stated earlier, most antidiscrimination statutes cover three general areas:

- *Discrimination in the Workplace*—(1) When an employer refuses to hire you because you have a disability, or you inform your current employer that you are disabled with HIV and he fires you. (2) When your employer refuses to offer *reasonable accommodation* to your disability. "Reasonable accommodation" is not an absolute term; it may vary with the circumstances. But your employer is required to try to accommodate your disability if your disability allows you to continue functioning as an employee. If, however, you can no longer do your job, your employer will not be found to be discriminating if he or she hires someone to replace you, or cannot create a way for you to do your job, given your disability. (3) When your employer, upon discovering your disability, begins acting in a manner, or causing others to act in a manner, that is intended to make you feel uncomfortable or discourage you from continuing to work. This may be done by moving your desk to a room by itself, cutting off your contact with the public, or other behaviors or methods that, taken together, form a pattern that would indicate that you are being singled out and treated differently than others because of your condition. This latter category may be more subtle and difficult to prove.

- *Discrimination in Housing*—(1) When a landlord who is informed of your disability or believes you to be disabled refuses to rent to you. (2) When a landlord asks you to leave your home after learning of your diagnosis. (3) When, as in an employment situation, a landlord engages in a pattern of behavior the object of which is to make you feel uncomfortable enough to leave the premises, by singling you out in some way. Housing discrimination, however, is not when a landlord moves to evict a tenant for nonpayment of rent, even if the tenant is a person with a disability. Some cities have programs to assist people with disabilities who are threatened with eviction but the action of the landlord is not discriminatory, because his motivation for eviction is not borne out of a desire to discriminate but to receive payment of rent, the same demand made on any tenant.

- *Discrimination in Public Accommodation*—To settle what is discrimination in this setting, it is necessary to determine what a public accommodation is. Some forms of public accommodation are obvious, a public transportation system, for example. If a bus driver refuses you service because you have HIV, this is a clear denial of access to public accommodation. But what about insurance? Can insurance be a public accommodation? It would appear that before 1990, the answer to this question would have been in the negative. Similarly, is treatment by a doctor a public accommodation? Again, before 1990, the answer would have been "no," depending on where you lived and what your local law may say. But with the advent of the ADA, public accommodation may include both your right not to be discriminated against in the insurance setting by being treated differently as a class of persons and your right to health care. This is a very broad category and its limits may not have yet been discovered by case law. If you think you have a case involving discrimination in a service or business setting, consult with a legal services program or local antidiscrimination office to see if you can use the ADA.

If the act or pattern of acts you perceive have caused you to be discriminated against have not occurred within the above contexts, then you may find that you have not been discriminated against in a manner that the law would consider illegal.

DO I HAVE A CASE?

People with AIDS, more than any other disease-specific group, are activists about their condition. They are activists on a political level, a medical level, and a personal level. They have come out into the streets and into the offices of senators, congresspeople, state assemblymen and women, and city councilors to lay out a clear agenda to protect their rights and public health. On a personal level, when face to face with a doctor, a person with AIDS tends to know more about his or her condition than patients with other illnesses. And on a personal level, generally speaking, there is more of a statement made about the ways by which a person wishes to be referred and the ways that are not appropriate ("Do not call me 'AIDS victim,' I am a person living with AIDS"). To a great degree, the depth of this activism on all levels is borne from a very strong anger at what is happening to the person with HIV and to his or her friends and family. There is a great deal of anger connected with any life-threatening situation, and one that is long-term simply serves to compound that anger. In turn, that anger has specific needs—to be noticed, to be vented, and to be used to create change in an environment that is fearful, sometimes hostile, and doesn't understand what it is like to be told you are dying at the age of 35.

Given this environment, a lawyer helping you to bring a discrimination suit must understand the complexities of your world. In the words of Schulman, "In some respects, the intermixing of people's psychological needs and people's legal rights and duties is something that I think any sensitive lawyer must always be aware of." It is a delicate balance to ascertain whether or not the case you are seeking to bring to court is going to be worth it to you.

David Schulman is a very adept and sensitive attorney. In his position since 1986, he has had the opportunity to review hundreds of legal discrimination claims. Doing so led him to a surprising discovery. Sometimes, in helping complainants through the sensitive discussion about their legal cases, he found that they reached the conclusion for themselves that they had not been discriminated against, but that they simply needed someone to talk to about how they felt about what was happening to them with their disease.

"Sometimes," says Schulman, "upon completing an investigation, I concluded that there was no discrimination, that instead what was occurring was that the person with AIDS was misperceiving job actions that were legitimate."

Schulman explains what causes this perception: a person with AIDS, very understandably, is perceiving his experience through a lens of a person inside a social standing that he or she knew vast numbers of people in society stigmatized." Schulman characterizes it in very concrete terms. He says that people with AIDS know that other people sometimes see them with a big "Kick Me" sign on their backs and that people do, in fact, kick them. Hospitals, doctors, nurses, bosses, friends, and family all at some time kick them, because they are now different, because they now have a stigma. "Therefore," says Schulman, "it is completely understandable that they would be more acutely sensitive to challenges to their professionalism or to their competence, and so run the risk, occasionally, of misperceiving others' actions as being AIDS discrimination when, in fact, there may be no discrimination at all." Sometimes, he concludes, all people want is respect, and that is what they have gotten from coming to his office. "I have to say that saying that leaves me feeling very mixed," he says, "because it is wrenching to deduce that such simple acts of human respect are so rare, but that seems to be the case."

In short, it is sometimes a fine line to determine whether or not an employer or service provider is treating you differently because you have AIDS and he or she is discriminating against you, or whether, in fact, you are reacting out of anger that you have AIDS or out of some denial that in fact there is a diminishment in your ability to do your job, a very painful thing to face. Sorting all this out is not the easiest thing on earth, either psychologically or legally. You should consider these questions:

1. Is your case well documented?
2. Does the nature of your discrimination fall within one of the three categories that are generally covered by antidiscrimination efforts: employment, public accommodation, and housing?
3. What are your motivations and what is your goal in bringing a case? Many times the remedy is reinstatement to the job with back pay. Is that what you want?
4. Did you ask for reasonable accommodation or did your employer offer you reasonable accommodation?
5. Are you sure that there was discrimination?
6. Do you have access to legal help?
7. Do you know what the laws are where you live regarding AIDS discrimination or discrimination against a person with a disability or handicap?
8. Do you feel that you want to do this, and are you prepared possibly to lose your case?

Getting Help on Discrimination

As outlined above, it is important to lay the groundwork for an actual case on discrimination carefully. This is often a focal point for a great deal of emotion and anger on both sides. To appear credible and to bring a successful suit, it is vital that there be an effort to set aside emotions that have nothing to do with the actual discrimination. In most high HIV-incidence states, there is likely to be a state office that is the division of human rights, or an equivalent thereof. In some metropolitan areas, there may be municipal human rights agencies of the city government, or they may be part of the city attorney's office. In the event of any suspected discrimination, these offices should be contacted directly.

In fact, where you go for help may depend largely on what kind of case you are bringing and what statutory protections are available to you. In New York City, for instance, one can avail oneself of the city antidiscrimination law, the state antidiscrimination law, or federal protections. The fact that all three exist may seem largely redundant to some, but, in fact, they comprise a very complete web of protections, as not every law can cover all of the citizens in every situation. For example, a postal worker in Brooklyn cannot, if suffering from discrimination, use the city or state law because neither the city nor the state can tell the federal government what to do. Therefore, that postal worker must use federal protections under the Federal Rehabilitation Act or the Americans with Disabilities Act. Someone in rural New York might only be able to use state law, particularly if his place of employment is so small that it is not covered by the Americans with Disabilities Act. In New York, in all three instances, there is help available, but the type of help may vary. The city and state law provide that the city and state offices will help you file your claim and that in an HIV case the matter is expedited. With respect to federal assistance in an ADA proceeding, the speed with which the matter is heard may vary from jurisdiction to jurisdiction, and, most definitely, the nature of the federal administration will determine the sympathy and speed with which HIV claims are heard. Assistance in this regard may be largely nonexistent and may require that you get your own attorney.

And that is often the rub with justice. It often appears that the only people who can access the system are those who can afford it. But because enforcement at the local and state levels is often administrative, the course through which you must steer your litigation is often simpler. In many cases, if a person cannot afford an attorney, the office of human rights will act as an advocate on behalf of the plaintiff. Administrative proceedings may be shorter and less formal than for a regular court case and, as in New York, there may even be an expedited process whereby the case is moved along at a faster pace. If you need an attorney for a case under the ADA and cannot afford one, check the resources available with a local AIDS community-based organization or with the local chapter of the American Bar Association.

There are also legal societies that provide aid and assistance to those in need.

Is It Worth It?

This is a question that cannot be bottom-lined for you. It is a question that can only be determined by you—the person bringing a discrimination suit. There is a burden in connection with bringing any litigation, and that burden can be heavy and stressful. Even if you win, the effort may not be worth it. In every discussion with lawyers involved in putting together this book, each one made some reference to the fact that litigation is a nasty business, to be seen only as a last resort. It is not as neat and compact as it may appear to be in films or television. David Schulman, who speaks with the background of a prosecuting attorney, offers counsel contrary to what people might think: "I can say that I know that litigation is unhealthy for any living thing, let alone someone whose major piece of medical advice is to lower their stress level. In some ways, the legal system is just all wrong for taking care of the legal needs of people with AIDS."

Before going through with any litigation, you have to make sure that it is what you want. Like any task, set a goal that your litigation will fulfill; make sure you can identify what it is that you want out of the lawsuit. Then acknowledge all that you will have to do to attain that goal: getting legal representation, submitting evidence, negotiating with the other side, possibly undertaking depositions, suffering expense, and bearing innuendo and scrutiny that will be deeply personal and, at times, unfair. It will be a long process, even if the jurisdiction in which you bring the case has an expedited method for handling HIV discrimination.

After you have acknowledged all the sacrifice that will be necessary, then only you can weigh the burden of bringing the suit on the scales of justice against your goal. If your goal is worth it, you will know.

There was a man named Vincent Chalk who taught school in California. He had HIV and he was discharged. He sued and won his case, but only after exhausting appeals were made. However, his case set a precedent for HIV in the workplace. Mr. Chalk took his case all the way because the principle was very important. As the litigant of his case, however, Mr. Chalk had to weigh what his desire to win his suit meant to him and to others against what it would cost both him and his family. For Mr. Chalk and for countless others, bringing the case was worth it. But it is important to keep in mind that not everyone's case is going to set a precedent and not everyone will win. Because there are so many emotional factors involved when one is discriminated against, it is a good idea to listen to the opinions of the people around you who may see things more objectively than you do. And above all, listen to the counsel of sensitive and enlightened lawyers you talk to about it; that is why they went to law school.

Perhaps the best way to make it worth it is to not let it happen at all. It is a fact that most lawsuits need never happen if one just goes out and does something preventive rather than wait for disaster to happen. "I think the single most important set of legal understandings that an HIV-infected person should learn is the idea of what I call an HIV legal checkup," advises David Schulman. "I think we have to make a sea change when it comes to protecting the legal rights of HIV-infected people. So many legal problems that people with HIV face, especially in the workplace, can be prevented if they are anticipated and planned for rather than reacted to after the problem arises." Schulman thinks that when people first test positive, there should be a course of action that they undertake, one that includes attending to legal needs. "The first thing people should do when they learn they are positive is to find friends and family who will give them unconditional support and love; the second thing they should do is they see a competent, knowledgeable physician; and on the third day, they should see a competent and knowledgeable HIV lawyer to give them the legal version of a medical checkup. I think," he says, "that this is the key."

In many ways, the idea of a legal checkup is like taking a prophylaxis drug to prevent pneumocystis pneumonia. Schulman believes that with the proper counseling from an HIV-competent lawyer, suits about discrimination could be lessened dramatically because you would know what to say and how to say it in a way that would create a safer environment for you in the workplace. The timing for informing an employer and the way in which it is done may make all the difference in the world. Anyone feeling confused or in doubt about how, when, or whether to tell an employer should seek as much input as possible and advice from persons experienced in workplace issues at AIDS community-based organizations.

CONCLUSION

The law does not respect irrational behavior that may result in the discriminatory treatment of a person with AIDS. The lack of toleration the law has for such treatment is based not only on our sense of justice but also on our public health policies. But the fact that discrimination is against the law doesn't mean it will ever stop. Discrimination is generally not borne out of a desire to be mean; it comes from a place of fear and from a need to feel safe in the face of danger.

And, while there have been great strides in fighting discrimination through the enactment of laws that forbid discrimination and provide remedy, a person with HIV still has to gain access to the legal system, something not always easy to do. There are networks of legal organizations, but many are overwhelmed or too small to handle the volume of cases they may have.

In addition, a lawsuit may not be the most appropriate thing for you as a person who may have experienced discrimination. You have to walk it through. You have to determine (1) whether you have suffered an injury because of someone's discrimination; (2) whether or not you want to seek remedy; and (3) whether seeking the remedy is going to be worth it to you.

You also have to decide what you want out of it. What is your objective? Does the law offer you what you want and need? You are going through something complicated and historical and at the same time uniquely personal. David Schulman has discovered through his years of AIDS mediation that one of the things that stands out is that there is a real value to preserving the relationships one has with others, and, in many instances, that is why people want to bring a discrimination suit. For example, in the context of employment, a person's job is a part of himself or herself and is at the very core of self-esteem. Neither the salary, nor the benefits of the workplace are as important as the knowledge that you are part of a team, that there is continuity to your life, and that you are with other people. This is very valuable and not, Schulman notes, something that the legal approach readily recognizes or is equipped to remedy. The legal system today looks at preserving rights, while Schulman, through mediation, takes a nontraditional approach in his role to battle discrimination, preferring to work to preserve relationships.

"I always felt that what I offered wasn't enough," he says. "I had to train myself to recognize that the processes I created were valuable to people too, not just the results. That is a very difficult idea to maintain, because you have to guard against being complacent and thinking the relationship is enough. It is not enough. Justice is what's enough. Nothing less than justice is what's enough."

Steps and Resources

- *Step*—examine what has happened to you carefully to determine whether the discrimination you suffer is (1) illegal, and

(2) part of a pattern of treatment rather than an isolated incident
- *Step*—determine what your goal is in seeking to redress any wrong you may have suffered
- *Step*—gather together any and all documentation of the events that led to the discriminatory act or support your claim
- *Resource*—Lambda Legal Defense and Education Fund, a national organization committed to achieving full recognition of the civil rights of lesbians, gay men, and people with HIV/AIDS through impact litigation, education, and public policy work, is headquartered in New York with offices in Los Angeles and Chicago. Lambda has regional and national expertise in all aspects of sexual orientation and HIV-related law and policy
- *Resource*—Legal Aid Societies in your jurisdiction
- *Resource*—local AIDS community-based organizations
- *Resource*—your city or state Office of Human Rights

6

The Most Precious Thing

Insurance

*If there were two birds sitting on a fence, he would
bet you which one would fly first.*

Mark Twain
*The Celebrated Jumping Frog
of Calveras County*

In his response to President Clinton's 1993 State of the Union
Address, which called for universal health-care coverage for all
Americans, Senator Robert Dole of Kansas made the statement,
"There is no health-care crisis in America." At the time, over 37
million Americans were without health insurance. Later, in August
1995, the *New York Times* stated that estimates of the number of
uninsured people had swollen to 43.4 million, with an annual
increase of approximately 1,200,000 people. Senator Dole's statement reflects just how far the debate on health care has left the
realm of public health and entered the arena of politics, stripping
the ideal of health-care reform of its valor.

The bone of contention in the debate on health-care reform is
the issue of insurance. The terms "socialized medicine" and even
"nationalized insurance program" all have very negative connota-
tions, not for health reasons but for political ones. Because the issue
is politically polarizing, it is often fraught with emotion, especially
around the notion of what our rights are with respect to health care.
While this is political and not a legal focus with which to begin a

discussion on insurance, it is important to understand the key role politics has had in shaping access to health care in the United States.

Further, it should be noted that the political debate on insurance reform has very little to do with philosophical principles centered on the ways we should get our health care. Rather, the polarization occurs as a result of the economics of health care. Inherent in any discussion of insurance is the fact that insurance companies are private concerns engaged in the business of "betting" that an event—an illness, a disability, damage from a natural disaster—will not occur. An insurance company is not a societal mechanism. An insurance company has investors who entrust the board of directors with their money in order to make more money and expect to be repaid with a premium on their investments. Companies do this by selling policies for premiums to consumers, either to you as an individual or to you as one of a group of individuals buying insurance through a pool, such as you may have through your employer. The premiums charged to you and the money received from investors is combined to back up the assurances made in the policy itself. This means that, in the case of health insurance, the insurance company guarantees that there is enough money to pay all or an agreed-upon portion of your medical bills. In doing so, the insurance company manages a balancing act between competing interests.

On the one hand, insurance companies are private businesses and are not dedicated to righting the wrongs in our society or even our system of insurance. As businesses, insurers must do the following:

- They must price their product competitively so that you or your employer will buy it. If the premiums are too high, then you will go to another insurance company for its policies.
- They must design the insurance coverage so that the benefits offered in their policies do not incur a cost factor that will make the sale of policies unprofitable.

- They must discriminate in order to survive. They can only sell their product to people, or groups of people, who will pose the least risk; otherwise, there is the possibility that a company will have to pay out more than it can take in.

The bottom line is this: if the proposition of providing insurance policies to people becomes financially unattractive, there is no point in investors giving any money to insurance companies at all, meaning that the company will not be able to afford to back up its policies. While all types of insurance are important, the existence of health insurance is an integral part of our entire health-care system. Oftentimes, given the emotional tenor of the debate on the issue of AIDS and insurance, the fact that companies are private business entities in existence to make a profit is often obscured.

Balanced with that identity, however, is the fact that any corporation is also a corporate citizen. It must behave in a responsible manner that is in the best interests of society—to ensure that its activities do not cause harm and, in fact, operate for the good of society. Given that reality, we have to determine the balance between the rights of the private corporation on the one hand and the interests of society at large in maintaining a healthy population.*

The AIDS epidemic has raised key questions about our health-care system that may have been asked before, but now have a new urgency. Access to health care in the United States, long before it was the 1992 election year topic or a presidential crusade, was an obvious and glaring problem for people in America, where so many millions live without insurance. The sheer number of uninsured people makes the matter of insurance coverage a critical issue. Additionally, with the advent of the HIV epidemic, there sprang into existence an entire new, and growing, population of people

*There have been studies that suggest that those people who are HIV positive and who have had to rely on government-sponsored insurance have higher mortality rates than those people with HIV who are privately insured. In one such study, released in 1993 at the annual meeting of the American Federation for Clinical Research, uninsured patients had a median survival period of 868 days compared to 1012 days for the privately insured. The median rate was defined as the number of days from diagnosis to mortality.

who found themselves in need of intensive and chronic medical care on which their very lives depended.

Perhaps one of the most interesting ironies about insurance in the era of an epidemic like AIDS is the obvious question not really addressed in the campaign to reform health care. If insurance companies providing health insurance can only be profitable by insuring those people who pose the least risk to them, then they will only be able to insure the healthy elite, leaving the burden of caring for the chronically ill to society at large and to the government and, consequently, the taxpayer.*

The issue is complicated further by preconceived notions and feelings about AIDS and those it has affected. Homophobia and racism figure greatly into the equation, causing some ambivalence in policy and legislative circles. As a result, the exclusion of people with HIV from insurance is a more accepted practice than it might be if AIDS had affected other populations. After all, it is reasoned, if all people with HIV were insured, premiums would have to rise accordingly.

However, the way society has dealt with issues of exclusion and HIV testing may have set a dangerous precedent for the future. If, as medical and genetic science advances, the medical establishment is able to test for genetic tendencies among insurance applicants—markers for those who are likely to come down with cancer, or Alzheimer's disease, or any of a host of other expensive illnesses—then insurance companies may only insure the healthy elite. What, then, will be the societal need for insurance at all? In fact, will private health insurance be rendered obsolete?

BACKGROUND

Mark Scherzer, an attorney in New York City with a private practice, specializes in insurance issues, particularly those related to

---

*In fact, the number of people who have insurance in the United States is decreasing. At the end of 1993, the *Wall Street Journal* reported that there were 38.9 million Americans who were uninsured, an increase over 1991 of 2 million people and up 4.2 million people from 1989.

insurance and HIV. Much of his experience at this came as a volunteer at the Gay Men's Health Crisis since the early 1980s, when he learned firsthand of the breadth and depth of problems faced by people and their insurance companies when it was discovered that the insured had AIDS. Since that time, he has seen old problems fade away while new ones surfaced. The fact that the epidemic produced new populations of people with HIV, the fact that people were living longer and consuming more care and therefore dollars, along with the fact that new medical treatments and drugs were burgeoning, all produced a complex set of problems that made conflict between the companies and the insured an inevitability.

Scherzer is able to characterize the evolution of these complexities in simple terms: "I think that in the first decade, we saw problems that were more related to an illness that suddenly appeared in a group of young people who were not prepared for it." Young and healthy people were leading a good life, and insurance planning didn't enter into it as a priority. Consequently, when they became catastrophically ill, they were unprepared, says Scherzer. "A tremendous part of my practice was then dealing with people who suddenly found out they had a health problem, purchased insurance without giving full disclosure about their health, and then were dealing with the fallout when the insurance companies tried to get out of the deal."

Even those people with HIV who were insured found that their access to health care was not what they thought it was once they actually went to use their insurance. It was not an uncommon experience to find that one's insurance company, which had appeared to offer coverage that was solid and secure, was no longer cooperative when it was discovered that a catastrophic illness was involved. People lost their insurance, found that they were unable to obtain coverage, discovered that their company decided to impose an "AIDS cap" on the amount that would be covered for an HIV condition—though they did not so for other catastrophic illnesses—and even discovered that some insurance companies tested people for HIV without their consent or knowledge.

While antidiscrimination statutes were undertaken by increasing numbers of jurisdictions in the United States to protect access to public accommodation, housing, and employment, there grew a kind of discrimination that remained legal, against which the law would do little. By the very nature of their business, the purpose of insurers is to discriminate. In fact, the better at discriminating they are, the better the business standing of the company.

While it is understandable that the very nature of the industry is to insure people with low risk of costing money to the company, the fact is that in the early days of the epidemic, insurance companies, frightened by the potential magnitude and costs of the HIV epidemic, engaged in some practices against people with HIV that would make victims out of people who sought to be otherwise. As mentioned in Chapter 5, people with HIV early on made clear a desire not to be labeled as victims, implying a total loss of control, but to seek empowerment in their struggle. However, in the face of a powerful industry, a person with a compromised immune system more likely than not became a victim.

"I see less of that in the second decade," says Scherzer. "We're seeing the demographics shift in who is being affected by AIDS." Consequently, there are corresponding shifts in the nature of the insurance problems that have developed. "The issue today is one of access to state-of-the-art treatment, planning issues, how people can plan to keep their benefits if going out on disability or changing jobs—transition issues." In essence, these issues, ones that involve planning and methods by which one goes onto disability, reflect a normalization of AIDS in the second decade.

HEALTH INSURANCE—ACCESS AND MAINTENANCE

There are three primary obstacles for people with HIV and insurance—getting insurance, keeping it once you have it, and making it work for you.

Access

Getting insurance can largely depend on the kind of insurance one wants to get. The types of insurance most commonly of concern to people with HIV are health, disability, and life. Disability and life insurance are both types of insurance that, because of their heavy financial payout and potential for fraud, are guarded more jealously than health insurance. Disability and life insurance are viewed as commodities that are available to those who can afford them and are prudent for people to own.

On the other hand, health insurance, by its very function in protecting quality of life and contributing overall to the good of public health, is viewed by an increasing number of people as something that is not a privilege but a right. Society has a moral, if not financial, interest in creating conditions that promote good health. Consequently, in the matter of health insurance, there are things that people with HIV can do to obtain insurance after a diagnosis of HIV, but there are virtually no ways for a disabled person to obtain disability and life insurance that do not involve a misstatement of fact.

With respect to health insurance, access also depends on the type of insurance coverage you are going to get, either an individual policy or a group policy. There are four primary types of health insurance.

Self-Insured Companies

This does not refer to people who buy their own insurance but rather to companies that provide their own insurance without going to an insurance company. You may work for an employer that is so large that, rather than buy insurance for all of its employees, will insure its employees itself. While other types of insurance are regulated by the department or commission for insurance in your state, self-insured companies are regulated by federal law, the Employee Retirement Income Security Act (ERISA). The interpretation of ERISA may be guided as well by the Americans with Disabilities Act (see Chapter 8).

Indemnity Insurance Plans

These are plans that were popular in yesteryear but today have the distinct disadvantage of being more expensive to the consumer. These plans allow you to choose any doctor or doctors. The plan will then reimburse you for all or, more likely, a portion of your expenses. These plans usually are accompanied by a deductible, meaning that you have to pay a certain amount of your health care cost before the insurer begins to pay.

Health Maintenance Organizations (HMOs)

These provide you with health care through their own facilities and physicians, and your choice of doctor is limited to those who are working for the organization, except perhaps under emergency circumstances. They are of lower cost to the consumer, and the copayment of office visits and prescriptions is usually minimal. There is no deductible. These types of plans have been growing in size and popularity, primarily due to their low cost. This is the fastest-growing type of insurance coverage in the United States.

Preferred Provider Organizations (PPOs)

These allow greater access to a wider variety of physicians than an HMO by allowing you to go to either (1) a doctor who is signed up with the PPO, resulting in low costs to you, or (2) the doctor of your choice, but with the consequence of higher costs to you if you go outside the preferred physician structure. Costs may vary, depending on how you use a PPO. A PPO offers you greater choice than an HMO, with a lower cost than an indemnity plan, but requires that you strategize your care proactively in order to get the most advantage of the situation.

HIV Testing—An Issue of Access

An obvious barrier to insurance for people with HIV is a requirement to test an applicant for antibodies to the virus as a condition for getting insurance. This is a practice that may vary widely from state to state and is done by health insurance companies to screen out individual applicants, not those on a group policy through employment. For life and disability insurance, this is a widely employed practice. Where antibody testing is not permitted, alternate testing such as T cell testing might be used. If you apply for an individual health insurance policy and the company requests an HIV test as a condition for a policy, you might contact your state department of insurance to determine whether this practice is acceptable within state regulations. If it is, you must choose carefully. Taking a test with an insurance company is inadvisable (see Chapter 8). Consider other ways to obtain health insurance, such as joining an employer where group insurance is provided, or, if you are HIV-positive and want an individual policy, determining whether your state offers high-risk pool insurance.

Once diagnosed with HIV or any life-threatening condition, getting insurance becomes immeasurably more difficult, but still not impossible, depending on the state in which you live.

High-Risk Pools

A growing number of states have developed high-risk pool insurance for their citizens. High-risk pool insurance is a state-subsidized type of insurance provided in most cases through an existing carrier, which basically makes it a business to insure the uninsurable.

The "uninsurable" are people with chronic conditions that are costly. People with heart trouble, cancer, diabetes, or HIV all would have trouble acquiring insurance on their own. But with high-risk pool insurance, insurance is made available as long as the consumers can afford it. To become a member of a high-risk pool insurance plan, one has to prove one's uninsurability—not usually a problem.

Rejection letters from a few insurance companies could do the trick. But the premium for high-risk pool insurance, like the risk, is high. Premiums can be 150 percent to 300 percent of the normal premium. Nevertheless, it is insurance, and if one can afford it, it is worth getting.

A word of caution about the future of high-risk pools, however. In cost cutting and budget balancing zeal, these pools may become targets, as they never make money despite their higher premiums. Therefore, there may be caps placed on the coverage, or access to the pools may be restricted to a set number of persons, and therefore, there may be a waiting list.

Hazard Signs—What to Avoid

In gaining access to health insurance, there are some pitfalls for people who are HIV-positive. Whether getting access by individual application or by group, there are safeguards built into coverage so that the insurer can control the risk associated with issuing policies. Particularly in the early part of the epidemic, these were common trouble spots for people with AIDS. With the growing influence of managed care systems in the health-care arena, there is less involvement of these issues than in yesteryear. But they are still factors today and explain some of the barriers to access for health insurance.

Material Misrepresentation—Insurance by Individual Application

One way to obtain insurance is to apply directly to a company as an individual. Individual coverage, as a general rule, is not as advantageous to you as group coverage, where risk is spread. Because the risk is focused solely on you, the applicant, the company wants to know a great deal about you, your habits, and your medical history before it decides to take a risk on you.

The primary way in which an insurance company can guard itself against fraud is by inserting a clause into the contract of insurance that states that if the applicant has omitted or falsified any health fact in the application, then the company reserves the right to cancel the policy and return the premiums. That is, the policy is cancelled because of a *material misrepresentation*.

If a person develops a medical condition that he or she wants covered, the ability simply to purchase an individual plan of insurance is compromised.

> Example: John Doe is uninsured. After a mild heart attack he goes to an insurance company for a policy. In response to the question about any history of a heart condition, John either leaves the answer blank or checks off "none." Within the first two years of the insurance contract, the applicant has another, more severe heart attack. This second heart attack is going to put him in the hospital for several days. The insurance company will then examine John's medical record with a fine-tooth comb to find any inconsistency between the application made for the insurance and the actual medical history. Once found, the company can rightfully claim material misrepresentation, cancel the contract of insurance, and return the premiums that John paid.

The standard by which a question of any material misrepresentation is measured is whether or not the omission of fact, or the falsification of an answer, would have caused the insurance company to have refused the insurance policy had it known the true set of facts. In the above example, if the company had known of the first heart attack, it most likely would not have issued the policy to the applicant, or, if it had, would have limited the policy in such a manner that it would not cover any heart ailment. This protects the company against fraud. It should be noted that it is irrelevant whether or not the applicant for insurance intended to deceive the company. An omission of fact is just as potent for dissolving the contract of insurance as a commission of fact.

With the advent of AIDS, however, insurance companies gave an entirely new meaning to the "material" portion of material misrepresentation. People who had private disability or health insurance policies often found that they were without insurance because of an omission, but one which no one would have otherwise characterized as material. One gentleman in New York had had acupuncture on his back for purposes of stress before he had applied for his disability policy. Within two years of getting his policy of insurance, the man was diagnosed with AIDS. When he put in a claim of disability, the company stated that the fact that he failed to write in the acupuncturist experience caused it to issue the policy, whereas it otherwise would not have done so. The company asserted that the misrepresentation was material to its decision to issue the policy in the first place. The fact that the misrepresentation was not material to the disability suffered by the insured was of no consequence. The company maintained, and won based on its claim, that if it had known that the man had had a back problem, it would never have issued the policy of disability insurance.

Should an insurance company discover a material misrepresentation, it will, in all likelihood, rescind the policy. A rescission means that the policy is treated as though it never existed for all intents and purposes. This means that the company will return to the expolicy holder all premiums paid on the policy. Rescission, it should be noted, is different than a cancellation by your company. Cancellation means that the insurance company is no longer covering the policy holder, and in that case premiums are not returned. If you are canceled by your company, you must determine the reasons for your cancellation and seek the assistance of your state department of insurance to determine whether or not such cancellation is warranted.

If your policy is rescinded, the implication is that you committed a material misrepresentation, or at the very least, the insurance company believes that you did. Look to see what condition the company believes you omitted from your insurance application, and check your medical records. Do this *before* cashing the check sent by the company rescinding your policy. Cashing the check may imply that you agree with the findings of the insurance company and acquiesce to the rescission. In addition, look at your policy to determine the term of *contestability*. This period of time will vary from state to state, but generally will run from two to three years.

The period of contestability means that the insurance company must have found the inconsistency for which the policy is being rescinded within an established time from the purchase of the policy. If the two-or three-year time period has lapsed, rescission of the policy may not be an option for the insurer.

Preexisting Condition—Insurance by Employment

The most common way for people to be covered by health insurance is when an employer has had the option of providing health-care benefits to its employees negotiated with insurance companies. Such contracts for insurance are purchased by a company for its employees who are carried as a group. For the insurer, when people are brought together in a large group, the risk associated with each individual in the group is lowered.

Protection from too much liability is built into the policy by the insurance company in the form of a preexisting condition clause. It is customary for each contract for insurance to have such a clause. A *preexisting condition* clause states that the individual insured shall not be covered for any condition that he had, or should have reasonably known that he had, at the time the policy began. The term for such a clause varies, sometimes built on a formula using the date of last treatment by a physician or by the date when the insured last filled a prescription that was a treatment for the condition. In other cases, the term for the clause is simply a set number of months, usually ranging from six months to a year. The result for the insured is that should he or she seek treatment for a condition that existed before, then the company will not pay for it.

> Example: John Doe has a mild heart attack while working for the Widget Corporation, where he has worked for twenty years. He enters the hospital and is treated. The group insurance plan that covers John pays for his hospitalization and treatment. When he returns to work, John is called by a placement firm with a job he has always wanted to have. He resigns from the Widget Corporation to take a job with a new company. The company offers excellent benefits but John is covered under a policy that has a preexisting condition clause

with a term of eleven months. After John has been with the new company for nine months, he suffers another heart attack and is hospitalized. This time the attack is more serious and may require surgery. John's coverage with his new company will not pay for the surgery, the hospitalization or anything to do with this second heart attack. John does not have the financial resources to pay for everything himself. The hospital may find that he is uninsured and no longer want his case. His doctor may feel likewise. The situation only exacerbates John Doe's condition. By virtue of the fact that John merely took the job he had always wanted, paradoxically, it is ruinous to his finances, his insurability, and his health. The hospital and the doctor may want to transfer John to a public facility that takes Medicaid. The problem there is that John has his life savings of $20,000, which he had put away for his first house. To be on Medicaid requires that John spend down his assets to poverty level.

This situation is not the fault of his new company. It is a hole in the safety net for people in the United States, where there is no national health insurance plan. Rather, the preexisting condition clause was a method by which companies protected themselves against people's getting onto a group insurance plan because they had gotten sick, not because they had wanted a job.

At one time, John Doe's plight occurred often. However, the ramifications for a person with HIV are even more serious. John Doe may not have experienced his second heart attack until a year after his employment with his new company. Then, the expenses associated with his condition would have been covered under the new policy. However, let's say that John Doe does not have a heart condition; he has HIV infection. While at the Widget Company, his physician started him on a regimen of antiretrovirals, such as AZT or DDI. John has 500 T cells. He gets the offer of his dreams and switches companies. Unlike the man with the heart condition, who may go the entire term of the preexisting condition term without getting treatment for his condition, the man with HIV cannot. He must take his prescriptives. He will have to pay for them during the entire preexisting condition clause and, should he experience any opportunistic infection, pay for that as well. Worse, if the preexisting condition term is built into the insurance contract as a formula, then John Doe with HIV may never be able to get out of the term, because he will not be able to stop his treatment.

As the example illustrates, there was a need for health care reform prior to the HIV epidemic. People fell through the cracks all the time. But with the epidemic, the number of people who would do so increased dramatically and, it could be argued, more irretrievably than anyone else.

Such things as preexisting condition clauses point up the fact that taking an HIV test has consequences beyond those that are medical. Once an HIV test is taken, if the test result is HIV-positive and the individual begins treatment with an antiretroviral, then the condition becomes medically documented. Once this happens, people may find themselves "job locked," unable to switch jobs because they would have to have their condition covered by a new insurance carrier. Almost everything has a loophole, however, and the exception to this rule is in the circumstance in which a person leaves employment with Company A and goes to Company B, which carries the exact same insurance as Company A. If there is no break in coverage, there may not be any resumption of the preexisting condition term. It is a small and unlikely loophole, but a loophole nonetheless. This is an important example of the fact that an HIV test has ramifications far beyond that of an ordinary medical test.

"Preexisting condition" traditionally meant just that, a condition one knew about or should have reasonably known that one had. However, with the advent of AIDS, this definition was stretched a bit by the insurance industry to go further. Complicated by the lack of scientific understanding as to how HIV impacted the immune system and just when a person developed AIDS, insurers began to classify any AIDS symptomology that occurred within the first months of being on a group insurance plan as being tied to a preexisting condition.

> Jane Doe, a person newly hired at Company A, which has a nine month preexisting condition term in its insurance contract, comes down with pneumocystis pneumonia, enters the

hospital, and gets a diagnosis of AIDS. Jane had had no idea that she was infected or that she was even at risk. During the first decade of AIDS, most people were diagnosed in this manner rather than after taking an HIV test and monitoring their immune system.

When Jane recovers after an expensive, three-week course of antibiotic therapy in the hospital, her claim is submitted to the insurance company. The company, seeing an expensive claim, comes back through her medical records and sees that the year before Jane had had a severe bout of the flu. Jane receives a letter from the insurance carrier for Company A informing her that her illness was a preexisting condition, tying her pneumocystis pneumonia back to her bout with the flu and maintaining that she knew, or should have reasonably known, that she had AIDS. The fact that 10 million other Americans also had the flu that year is not mentioned.

Jane is left in an unenviable position. Her hospital bill will most likely be several thousand dollars ($700 per day for 21 days, plus doctor charges). She may begin to get threatening letters from her hospital. Her doctor may even be upset with her. She may suffer anguish over the collection efforts of the hospital. She may be asked by her doctor to find another physician. She is upset, she is confused, she is threatened with her very lifeline, as her physician is her link to her antiretrovirals and prophylaxes for opportunistic infections. The result is that Jane has a lot on her mind, the least of which is her medical condition and how best to take care of herself.

Later, after the preexisting condition term expires, Jane will be covered. However, if her preexisting condition term is set on a formula, she will have a difficult time getting out from under it because she will always be getting medical treatment or taking an antiretroviral, such as AZT.

While Jane Doe becomes a victim, the other victim is the health-care industry. Jane will never be able to pay the hospital bill. The hospital will take a loss. Since Jane Doe is not unique in her circumstance, the cost of health-care dramatically begins to be impacted by the AIDS epidemic.

Jane could attempt to contest her claim in court. Unfortunately, in the 1980s especially, time was not on the side of the AIDS litigant, allowing insurers to act with some impudence without fear of being sued.

A bright note—with the growing influence of Health Maintenance Organizations, preexisting conditions are of less concern as they are usually covered when you join the HMO.

Capping

When the epidemic was first apparent, insurance companies could see that they were in for a potential loss of millions of dollars, both in health-care claims and in life insurance payouts as the result of a devastating and almost uniformly fatal illness. Among employers who self-insure their employees rather than purchase a contract of insurance through an insurance company, the financial peril was even more greatly perceived.

Insurance companies are able to spread their risk throughout a great pool of people. Employers who self-insure are only able to spread the financial risk through their own employees, thus making them more sensitive to a contagious, catastrophic, and expensive disease like AIDS.

To protect themselves from the potential losses, many self-insureds sought to cap their policies with respect to HIV treatment. In 1993, self-insured Storehouse, Inc., lowered its insurance coverage from $1,000,000 to $25,000 for employees with AIDS, reserving the right to amend their insurance coverage at any time. Likewise, the state of South Carolina amended its high-risk rool insurance plan, which insures people who have been unable to get private insurance, denying coverage to anyone with AIDS. The Allied Services Division Welfare Fund, representing over 20 companies across the nation, reduced the amount of benefits under its insurance plan to $5,000 despite the fact that the limit was $300,000 for other catastrophic illnesses. Likewise, the Mason Tenders District Council Welfare Fund in New York also tried to limit amounts paid with respect to AIDS. The result was inherently discriminatory and unfair. If an employee developed cancer, Alzheimer's, diabetes, or any other long-term chronic illness that would incur great expense, the cap on the payments made under the policy would be the same for everyone, perhaps $500,000 over one's lifetime. "However," said the self-insureds, "if you develop AIDS, we are going to limit the amount we will pay under the policy to $5,000." This sounds extreme, but it is exactly what occurred. All of these health funds were sued.

Insurance companies are governed by the insurance laws of each state, where the practice of capping would in all likelihood be prohibited by law. However, self-insured companies were regulated by a federal law, called the Employment Retirement Income Security Act (ERISA), which did not clearly forbid the practice of capping as illegal. Whether or not a self-insured company could create a disease-specific cap became an unclear legal issue. Even after the 1990 passage of the Americans with Disabilties Act, these funds sought to have disease-specific caps imposed since they did not conflict with ERISA.

The decision was not entirely obvious, from a legal point of view. The United States Supreme Court was not helpful in this regard when it refused to hear a case brought under ERISA challenging a cap that reduced coverage from $1,000,000 to $5,000 for HIV. The drop in coverage came only after the employee revealed his status to his employer. The refusal by the court appeared to lend strength to the position that such practices were not illegal.

While some lower courts initially sided with the health funds, stating that caps were permissible, in 1994 an appeals court in Massachusetts became the first to rule that these health funds were subject to the Americans with Disabilities Act, and uncertainty appears to have been dramatically diminished. The self-insurance provided by companies was deemed an accommodation by appeals courts for purposes of the act and therefore was covered by its prohibition of discrimination against persons with HIV disease. Although the ADA was passed in 1990, its effect on this area of insurance was not clear until much later, when cases brought under the act were heard and decided.

In the wake of these developments, funds have had to abandon the capping practice, as evidenced by a 1995 decree that awarded compensation to persons with HIV who had seen the Philadelphia-based Laborer's District Council, a joint union–management fund for construction workers, cap their coverage at $10,000 while leaving it at $100,000 for all other illnesses. After the decree, the cap with respect to AIDS was raised to the same level as all other diseases.

Again, the fact that a practice may be illegal does not mean that somewhere there isn't someone willing to try it. People who are told that their insurance coverage for AIDS is capped should seek legal redress immediately.

Maintenance

Once one is fortunate enough to get insurance, there must be a conscientious effort to maintain it. As part of the 1994 debate on health-care reform, an important component of the proposed coverage was one of "portability," the ability to take your coverage with you wherever you go. It is one of the few principles of health-care reform that seemed to win serious consensus among legislators and policy makers and is a growing factor in today's insurance industry. There are safeguards built into the system today to allow portability of coverage to you through life's changes. But they do not happen automatically; you need to watch the signposts and know which way to turn.

Many factors may affect portability. Keeping the insurance you have is an important, though sometimes seemingly complicated, accomplishment. Not everyone is on equal footing for keeping insurance. It may depend on where you work, what state you are in, what support you may get from governmental programs, and on what personal financial resources you have available to you.

Taking It with You—Conversion of a Group Policy

Assuming that you are fortunate enough to have been working for an employer who was able to provide you with health insurance coverage while you were working, you may get to keep the coverage. At the point at which you become disabled and need to leave your job, you have rights to maintain your health insurance or a form of it. In no case is the insurance maintained without your having to pay for it, though some states will have programs that may help you out in terms of being able to pay premium on a health insurance policy. Because the Medicaid that may be available in your state is a combination of federal and state funds, it is in the best interests of the state in which you live to see to it that you maintain your insurance. If you are privately insured and not using Medicaid, then the state saves money, and some states have reasoned that it is cheaper for them to pay the insurance premiums of the disabled than it is to pay for their care directly through Medicaid programs. This means that, if your state legislature has understood this, there may be support made available to you to pay your premiums.

Likewise, it has also been in the best interests of the federal government to respond to the growing needs of people with insurance who are disabled. Rather than have people leave their jobs in a disabled condition and lose their insurance, thereafter going onto the public system of health-care support, Congress enacted legislation designed to help people with disabilities maintain private insurance.

The Consolidated Omnibus Reconciliation Act (COBRA), passed in 1985, mandated that an employer permit a person who is leaving employment for any reason other than being fired for his own gross misconduct to maintain coverage on the group plan. In keeping the coverage, you as the employee must be able to make your own payment on the plan, which is a figure based on your own share of the group premium paid by your employer to the insurance company. There may be a slight additional charge that represents an amount you pay to your employer for handling the administrative aspect of your payments to the insurance company.

The law mandates that you may keep your position on the group plan for a period of 18 months, allowing then that you can leave employment on disability and stay with the coverage until such time as you qualify for Medicare (see Chapter 3).

The exceptions to COBRA are

- If you work for a religious organization or for an employer with fewer than 20 employees
- If your departure from employment is due to your own gross misconduct

Gross misconduct is not specifically defined under the law, but Mark Scherzer relates two cases that help clarify what constitutes gross misconduct. In the first one, which occurred in California, a woman told one of her fellow employees that she was "in trouble." To relate to others that you were "in trouble" constituted a violation of one of the employer's rules. For this breach of rules, she was discharged from her job. The court said that this behavior was not gross misconduct but merely an inadvertent violation of a rule that was done without intent to damage the employer. The court applied rules similar to those that relate to unemployment insurance. "You may screw up on the job, you may not do a task properly, or you may break a rule without intending to damage your employer and that may still not constitute gross misconduct," says Scherzer.

Scherzer points out the difference between misconduct and gross misconduct with a second story in which gross misconduct was found to have been committed by a woman working for a supermarket in Chicago. As part of a sales promotion, the supermarket distributed saver stamps, which could be redeemed for turkeys. The employee stole the stamps and then redeemed them for free turkeys. After she was discharged from her job, she developed cancer. She attempted to extend her insurance coverage under COBRA but her employer refused, saying that she had been guilty of gross misconduct. The court sided with the employer, stating that an act such as theft does constitute gross misconduct. "If you are going to do stuff like blow up the safe or sell the employer's trade secrets to competitors or steal stamps, then you're not going to get COBRA rights," says Scherzer. The difference is between performing an act that is a rule violation and one that actually inflicts damage and shows willful intent.

Your employer is under an obligation to notify you of your COBRA options within 45 days of your departure from employment. However, to be on the safe side, when you leave employment, ask for a description of your COBRA rights from your employer. Put this request in writing and keep a copy of the letter. If you want to be absolutely safe, send the request by certified letter, return receipt requested. Once your employer sends you the information (whether or not you receive it), then he or she has fulfilled the obligation and the clock begins to tick for you. You then have 60 days to decide whether or not you want to stay on the group plan. Your coverage will be effective back to the time when you left your employment. In short, elect COBRA coverage as quickly and efficiently as possible. Leave nothing to chance.

Individual Policy Conversion

Some states allow you to make an individual conversion of your group policy to an individual policy of health insurance. This is very different from COBRA, which allows you to stay on the group plan. Group insurance coverage is invariably much more economical and provides coverage for a far greater range of conditions and procedures than does an individual insurance policy. That is because the premium charged to a group policy is one based on the experience of a group of people, and the risk is spread out among the group. However, the amount of risk associated with an individual is higher and, therefore, the premium will reflect that increased risk, as will the coverage for various benefits under the policy. For example, prescription drug coverage may not be available to an individual, whereas it would be to the group, yet the charge of a premium per individual in the group is far less than the premium charged to an individual. Nevertheless, if you do not have a COBRA option, this may be your only avenue to health insurance.

In converting a policy from a group to an individual, you may be shocked by the cost to you and the reduced coverage available. However, you must weigh the policy's worth to you carefully. A policy of health insurance, even an expensive one, may prove to be the most valuable thing you own, and, like all precious possessions, it is expensive and should be maintained if at all possible. Each individual must judge for himself or herself whether or not it is worth it to keep an individual policy that may have extremely high monthly or quarterly premiums. But the existence of a policy may make the difference for you between access to care that is publicly funded and care that is provided by a private hospital, where the quality of your care may be so much higher that your care and even your life span can be dramatically impacted. Moreover, given the fact that having insurance grants you more options with respect to your care, you are placed in a position of having a greater measure of control by having insurance. When your insurance is cut off, your treatment options are narrowed.

Individual conversions are not all that common anymore given the advent of COBRA. Still, they can be useful where states have mandated them in situations where your employer is not covered by COBRA laws, that is, when there are too few employees in the business to allow the COBRA law from taking effect in your particular situation.

It is important to remember that COBRA is a federal law, affecting every state, while individual conversion laws are on a state-by-state basis, and you may or may not have individual conversion available to you. If it is available, the length of time that you may have before electing to convert to an individual policy will vary from state to state. Check with your state office of insurance to determine whether or not you have conversion rights and how long you have to elect such a conversion.

LIFE INSURANCE

To this point, most of what has been explained pertains primarily to health insurance. But life insurance has also become extremely important to people with HIV. It has been a venue for HIV testing and has become a resource for people through accelerated payments and viatical settlements. Though to a lesser degree than before, most people who are employed have a life insurance policy as part of a benefits package along with their health insurance coverage. Others try to get it after their diagnosis. There are several similarities to the issues outlined above regarding health insurance that affect life insurance. Many of the hazards that existed for health insurance are also present with life insurance, particularly regarding material misrepresentation about HIV status. There are also important differences from health insurance. For example, while it is illegal in many states to test a person for HIV before issuing a health insurance policy, it has been a longstanding practice for life insurers.

Life Insurers and Testing

Obtaining life insurance almost anywhere for almost any amount will require an HIV test. Restrictions on such practices are far less imposing than on health insurance. Life insurance is not about the greater public health; it is, in essence, a financial investment. The law is not going to guard jealously your right to apply for a life insurance policy that will put the insurer at greater risk than it is willing to undertake. Therefore, HIV-antibody testing as a prerequisite for a life insurance policy is not illegal in any jurisdiction.

A person interested in purchasing a policy of life insurance should be cautious because of the HIV antibody test. Taking a test is something that should be done when you decide to take it. It should be something you do for your health, not to satisfy someone else's curiosity. But that is just what taking a test with a life insurance company is about—taking the test as a prerequisite for the needs of a company over your own personal needs. Surely, one of the most inadvisable ways to take an HIV test is with an insurance company.

This is precisely the manner in which Magic Johnson reports that he discovered his HIV status. He related that his antibody status was discovered when, in the course of making an application for a life insurance policy, he underwent a blood test for HIV. This type of testing is, of course, by its very nature, not anonymous. Make no mistake, the insurance company will discriminate against you as a result of a positive test—you will not get your life insurance. If you are applying for individual life insurance, it is by all means advisable to have the test done first at an anonymous testing site or, if one is not available, through some confidential means of testing (see Chapter 8). One day, anonymous testing may be feasible in the home, allowing you to discover your own results first, then submit to a test by an insurance company. In any case, take the HIV test when you want to take it, not when someone else wants you to. You could do yourself more harm than good. The most cautious course is to test first at an anonymous test site, wait six months, and test again. If your test is negative both times, then apply for the life insurance policy.

Life Insurance and Beneficiaries

People involved in same-sex relationships often express concern about naming a nonfamily member as a beneficiary of a life insurance policy for fear that the company will not pay out. If Alice, a 35-year old woman, designates as a beneficiary Mary, also 35 and residing at the same address, Alice may believe that the insurance company will guess the true nature of their relationship and refuse to pay her lover should something happen. There is no reason that you should not name any beneficiary of your choosing when filling out the form. If a company attempts to put a restriction on the type of beneficiary you are naming, contact your state commissioner on insurance to determine whether such a restriction is sanctioned by law. If you are involved in a same-sex relationship and you want to make that person your beneficiary, simply write "friend" as the nature of the relationship.

While doing this may seem homophobic, it is not recommended to use the term "lover" when making such a designation. The only viable way for a beneficiary designation to be challenged successfully is to assert that a person was under undue influence when making the beneficiary election. Some conservative courts might interpret the spelling out of a same-sex union in the word "lover" to constitute an undue influence.

There should be caution also when electing to name your estate as the beneficiary of your life insurance proceeds. While this is perfectly legal, the money from your insurance policy then becomes subject to attack by any creditors you may have at the time of your death. Even if you have no such creditors now, you never know what conditions may exist at the time of your death. Rather, it is recommended that you name the beneficiary or beneficiaries on your statement with your insurance company. You can name more than one and assign percentages to each beneficiary. This makes the funds safe from attack by your creditors and gives the added benefit that your beneficiaries will receive the money much more quickly than if it were sent through an estate that would need to be probated (see also Chapter 1).

Premium Payment and Premium Waivers

Always, always, always pay your premiums on your life insurance policy. If you are late, there is a grace period provision that is contained in your policy. Read it and memorize it. However, it is also important to read the provision that discusses your premiums in the event of your disability. In that event, your premiums may be waived entirely for the duration of your disability. Your policy will also tell you how long you have after the onset of your disability to file for a waiver of your premiums.

Viatical Settlements and Accelerated Payments

One of the many things the AIDS epidemic has introduced to the legal world is the viatical settlement. While anyone can enter into one, viatical settlements, as they were devised in 1988, have primarily been used by people with HIV.

Viaticals get their name from the Latin word *viaticum*, which was a term applied to the blessing given to a person who was dying. Despite this cheery origin, viatical settlements have been the new wave in insurance. Since 1989, there has been a great deal of growth in this practice as a new sector of commerce, with over 50 firms participating by 1994 in what has become an industry worth several hundred million dollars.

While we traditionally think of life insurance as an investment made to provide for the future security of one's family or loved ones, viaticals allow one to cash in the benefit for oneself while one is still alive to enjoy it. Sometimes a broker is involved in the transaction, connecting the person with the life insurance policy with the viatical company. An application is made to the viatical company and the medical records of the insured are examined by physicians, who may advise the company as to the life expectancy of the applicant. Viatical companies vary on the amount of cash they will advance and on the number of years of life expectancy they will accept for their investment.

The deal sounds ghoulish. It also sounds easy. It doesn't need to be either. On its face, the settlement basically allows for the early cash-in of a life insurance policy. If you have a $50,000 policy, you may sell it for $40,000. The viatical company takes over the payment of the premiums on the policy. When you die, the investors get back their investment with a profit of $10,000.

There is a great deal of discomfort on the part of many persons with respect to viatical settlements, and the subject provokes controversy. Some feel it is immoral to allow people to invest in the death of other persons. Yet, in effect, that is what life insurance is all about in the first place. A company accepts your premiums, essentially betting that you won't die until they have made money off the money you pay them in premiums. A viatical is just another way of looking at it.

Still, others feel that companies that engage in viatical settlements need to be regulated. Currently, California, Indiana, Kansas, New Mexico, and New York are the only states known to regulate viaticals, though other states have legislation pending. The National Association of Insurance Commissioners has created a model statute for the regulation of viatical companies. In addition, the

Securities and Exchange Commission has brought suit against one viatical company in Texas, charging it with dealing in securities.

As a new industry, viaticals pose an interesting question for people with AIDS. There are certainly good arguments in support of viatical arrangements, which allow a person to reap the benefit of having invested in an insurance policy. The National Association of People with AIDS (NAPWA) has been an outspoken supporter of viatical arrangements, urging responsible regulation that does not prevent the marketplace from allowing persons to undertake such arrangements if they choose. William J. Freeman, executive director of NAPWA, cites a survey of people with HIV conducted by his organization, which revealed that the need for financial assistance is keenly felt. "Nearly 3 out of 10 respondents are living on less than $500 a month, and another 3 in 10 live on between $500 to $1000 a month. Over a third of those who work full-time say they still need financial assistance." The benefit of having the policy is not only for the possibility of enjoying life with more material relish but also for necessary care for people with AIDS, who may have lost other types of insurance or have been financially compromised early in their relationship with HIV. Psychosocially, the empowerment alone that might be experienced in gaining authority and control over one's financial resources may very well be a good enough reason to make a viatical settlement. As Freeman states, "We who advocate for the terminally ill want to preserve as much choice as possible for them." NAPWA's bottom-line position is that regulation to protect the consumer can and should be constructed but in such a way as not to inhibit the market.

But dealing with a viatical settlement may not be as easy or as cut and dry as it may seem. Negotiating with an unknown viatical company in an unregulated industry has significant risks. "There is a great deal of potential for abuse," says Mark Scherzer, who is able to cite examples. "People have entered into viatical agreements only to find that the check was not in the amount that was agreed on. It can be a rude shock." Clearly, you need to read the fine print. But it may be more than that. If a viatical company is late with a check, or if the check is not in the amount agreed upon, or even if the check bounces, you may have very little recourse if the industry is not regulated in your state. The New York statute regulating viatical companies calls for the money that the viatical company is putting up to purchase the policy to be placed in escrow when the agreement is signed. It is important to remember that viatical settlements are not regulated by the federal government but on a state-by-state basis. If you are in an unregulated state, there is no agency with which you can readily register a complaint. You may contact your superintendent of insurance or your state insurance commission, but there may be little that the office can do for you. You certainly may have a cause of action in civil court, but that may not be good enough because bringing and winning a lawsuit takes a great deal of time, effort, and resources. Some issues to consider before entering into a viatical arrangement include the following:

- Will the influx of cash interrupt any public benefits that you may be getting (see Chapter 3)? If you have already spent down your assets to qualify for Medicaid, you may become ineligible and have to spend down all over again.
- Is there a broker involved? If a broker represents himself as "fee-free," he may be getting a finder's fee from the viatical company.
- Are you getting the best price? Have you shopped around, gotten bids?
- Are you in a state that regulates viatical agreements? Call your state office of insurance to find out.
- What will the tax implications be? While the proceeds from a life insurance policy paid to a beneficiary would not be considered taxable by the Internal Revenue Services (IRS), viatical settlements are currently taxable. There may be state tax implications as well. As much as a third may go in taxes. However, many states will not tax the income from a viatical settlement, treating it as they would insurance proceeds.
- Are you sure that your insurance policy is not contestable by another party?
- Are there alternatives?

With respect to alternatives, Scherzer suggests that if there is the option, a person may choose to borrow the money from a friend or relative and thereafter make that friend or relative the beneficiary of the policy. In effect, this is a form of viatical settlement, only it is a private transaction. If this is a chosen alternative, however, the insurance policy must be secure and not subject to nonpayment by the company. For instance, if the policy was obtained under circumstances where the insured person made a material misrepresentation in his or her application to the company, the policy may never be paid by the company, and the friend or relative would be hurt by the financial loss. There is also often a provision contained in insurance policies for "accelerated benefit." An accelerated benefit is similar to a viatical in that the money comes during your lifetime, but it is not sold to a third party. Rather, the insurance company pays a portion of the policy to the insured during his or her lifetime. This procedure is not without its complications, it is not part of every policy, and it may require that the intended beneficiaries of the policy sign off on such an agreement before the company will go through with it. These are serious alternatives that should be investigated before entering into a viatical settlement with a company, particularly in a state that does not regulate the new viatical industry.

This is not to say viaticals are bad or good; they can be appropriate and even necessary. As Scherzer states, "They fill a void and have satisfied a need of many people who don't have adequate ways to go through a long-term disability; they are a necessary component. On the other hand, it disturbs me to see what purport to be the profit margins in the field. These companies say they are making huge returns, leading me to think it is not a competitive market and that people don't shop around adequately—and the consumer needs to have more power in the relationship."

Clearly, however, a life insurance policy is a premium commodity. As such, it should only be compromised under special circumstances or with great care. People who live in a state where there is viatical regulation should get all of the information about such regulation from their state commissioner or insurance office as well as determine from the state commissioner or superintendent of insurance whether there are any outstanding complaints about a viatical settlement company with which one is dealing.

DISABILITY INSURANCE

The rules for disability insurance largely resemble those for life insurance and health insurance with respect to access and maintenance. Most people who have disability insurance are getting it through an employer. Issues of access are governed along the same lines as those for health insurance. If you are part of a group, you receive the benefit of disability insurance. If you leave your employment, you may have the option of taking the disability insurance with you as long as you pay the premium, though this is not federally legislated in the manner that COBRA is for health insurance.

If you apply for a policy of disability insurance as an individual, you are subject to many of the same rules as with life insurance. You will also be scrutinized carefully in order to assess the risk attached with issuing you a policy, meaning that you may be subject to HIV antibody testing and a detailed application asking questions about your medical history. If you omit some of that history or change some of that history, you may find the policy rescinded.

Disability insurance is there to provide you with private income that will make up for the income you lose as a result of being unable to work. The income you get from your policy will usually fall subject to taxation, except for certain circumstances that are dependent on how the premiums were paid. If you have a disability policy through an employer, then you should check with your plan administrator to determine how best to pay for these premiums and whether or not it is possible for you to pay for the premiums in a way that will make the payments from the policy nontaxable. If your policy is an individual policy, your benefits may be subject to tax.

The objective of the policy is to pay you a set percentage of your former income, which is generally a level of 60 percent. In order to reach 60 percent of your former income, disability will take into account any support you may be receiving through entitlement programs (see Chapter 4) or through state programs of short term disability.

> Example: John Doe earns a salary of $4000 a month. He has a disabling event and applies for his benefit under the policy. At the same time, he applies for federal programs he has paid into and possibly even state programs. Let us say that his federal benefit is $500 per month and 60 percent of his former income is $2400. From his insurance company he will receive $1900 and from the federal program he will receive $500.

The disability payments will be retroactive to the time of the disabling event, and there is usually a waiting period that ranges from one to six months.

If you have already been diagnosed with a life-threatening condition such as HIV and you want to make an individual application for disability insurance, you will probably be unsuccessful. If you have received treatment of any kind, your condition is documented. The application for the disability policy will ask detailed questions about your health status. Omitting a fact such as HIV will only give the company cause to rescind the policy when, at a subsequent date, you put in a claim for disability based on HIV. Needless to say, the company will conduct a thorough investigation of your application and your medical history before paying on an expensive catastrophic claim. Once the discovery is made of your prior treatment, the company will consider that you have made a material misrepresentation and will rescind the policy. The only viable way for a person with HIV to obtain disability insurance is through employment.

CONCLUSION

For those who are diagnosed with a catastrophic illness and who are uninsured, there are limited options nevertheless available for getting health insurance that will help in the battle with illness. Remember, with the aim of maintaining as much control and authority over what is going on while you are facing a battle with HIV, having insurance affords one more options and therefore lets you exercise more control and authority over your situation. That does not mean that if you cannot get health insurance, or if you cannot possibly afford health insurance, you are doomed to an existence without control and authority, of illness and despair; it simply means that you may have to choose your medical options with great care.

Other kinds of insurance, disability and life insurance, are not options that are generally open for people with any catastrophic illness. If you didn't have these types of insurance before an illness, your chances of getting them afterwards are slight. Some people do get around some barriers by trying to hide the truth, but this is neither honest nor generally successful, and can, in the end, create more problems than it was intended to solve.

Steps and Resources

- *Resource*—State government. Each state has an office in the state capitol that regulates insurance, and the head of the office is either the state insurance commissioner or the state superintendent of insurance.
- *Resource*—Your local AIDS community-based organization. This organization may have lawyers or insurance experts or be able to make a referral for you.
- *Resource*—The media. Whatever your sexual orientation, check any local gay newspapers or a gay yellow pages if you live in a community where there are apt to be such resources. You may find gay insurance brokers advertised who will know a great deal about insurance matters and HIV.
- *Resource*—Federal government. If your insurance matter regards a self-insured company, you may need to contact the Department of Labor in Washington, D.C. at 202-219-6666.
- *Resource*—Brokers. In some cities, there may be professional organizations made up of gay and lesbian brokers. Look in local gay and lesbian papers in the classified section under "professional organizations" or call a local hotline to see if such an organization exists.

7

Ball and Chain
The Story of Bob

I am the spirit that always denies.
Johann Wolfgang von Goethe
Faust, Part I

What follows is an interview with a person with AIDS. His story is included because it illustrates so well so many aspects of life with AIDS. It is a story about a person who was so afraid of AIDS that there was no aspect of it he seemed willing to face. He was in denial. That denial, so natural for us all, carried a heavy cost for him, particularly with regard to his insurance coverage for disability. Bob's story is one that portrays the legal difficulties a person with HIV can have with respect to discrimination and insurance. It is also about personal challenges. Most of all, it is a story of love and courage, facing the phantoms, and discovering what life is all about.

It is a spring evening. Winter rains have caused Los Angeles to bloom as though it were a giant hothouse, and as the sun sets, flowers yield a scent that reminds people why, in spite of all the natural as well as the not-so-natural disasters, people move from all over the country to live here. Despite all the jokes about air quality in southern California, the air is clear and clean and cool.

The apartment building is in a quiet, middle-class neighborhood. A woman answers the door, inviting both a cat and me inside. She apologizes as she eats Chinese food from a Styrofoam tray; it is the only chance she has to eat on a busy schedule. Her name is Adele. She is a native Californian. She and I sit and chat for a minute, and then she calls upstairs to Bob.

It seems as though Bob is at first reluctant to join us. Adele calls to him a second time. He slowly comes down the stairs, and introductions are made. Adele comments that he should put something on his feet. Bob doesn't move, perhaps unsure whether he is going to stay. He is nice looking, quiet mannered, and cautiously shy. Perhaps putting on slippers would be to signal some sort of commitment to talking about AIDS, something he would rather forget entirely.

He begins to talk about himself, guardedly at first. His answers to questions are in short sentences. Bob is one of those people who moved from somewhere else to be in California. He was raised in a large family in the Midwest. He has a cousin who died of AIDS. He moved to California, having gotten a job with a four-star hotel chain, and worked as a purchasing manager for 10 years. Bob lives with Adele, whom he met at work. At some point, unnoticed, Bob puts on his slippers. He looks less wary.

In response to questions, Bob begins to talk more about his background and the fact that he has HIV. He is 33 years old, within the optimal age group of people with AIDS. He may have been infected in his early twenties, or even his late teens, the age at which most people think themselves invulnerable. Certainly with HIV, everyone wants to believe there is as much distance as possible between them and the epidemic. It is someone else's problem.

It became Bob's problem at Christmas in 1991, when he had trouble swallowing. The pain grew so fierce that he missed two weeks of work, and he found he couldn't eat anything. "I was swollen, and every time I ate something it was like I was chewing on broken glass," he said. He went to the doctor, who looked at his throat and told him that he had a very bad case of thrush, a fungus that can grow inside the mouth or even the lungs of a person with a compromised immune system. Thrush is a condition that can be more than annoying or uncomfortable. If left untreated, it can kill.

About that time, Bob met Adele. Adele is a counterbalance to Bob in almost every way. He is shy, retiring, reticent, and quiet. Adele is not. She is direct, energetic, outgoing, and very full of life and expressive. Bob is blond and fair; Adele is brunette and dark. Bob speaks in short, simple sentences; Adele speaks in sentences that are paragraphs. Bob is in denial. Adele faces everything head-on.

"When we met," says Adele, "we were friends and confidants at first. I knew a lot about his life. I don't know how it actually happened, because I always had a fear factor of this man. He was a manager and he was very particular and detail-oriented." Bob looks on, stoic and stern looking.

"I had been so intimated by him for the longest time, and then one thing led to another. He told me about his life and I told him about mine. We became friends." Adele appears as though she doesn't know that the word "denial" even exists in the English language. Bob appears to embody it.

At one point, Bob seems frustrated. "There is a part of the story that is missing here."

"You should tell him," says Adele.

"I was with a guy," he says, "and he died just this past year."

Bob found out that he was HIV-positive at the same time he found out that he had AIDS. He had never taken an HIV test, even though he was a gay man living in California in the beginning of the second decade of AIDS.

Adele explains his state of denial in this area. "If you knew Bob's history as a child. He was very much always the quiet one of his family. He wasn't the yeller, the screamer, or the fighter, he just always slipped through the cracks."

"I'm not a complainer," says Bob.

Bob's home is comfortable and airy. He has a cat and a dog, who seem to adore one another. The apartment looks comfortable. A good deal of thought has gone into it. But it is a home that Bob and Adele will shortly have to vacate because the landlord has managed to evict them on legal grounds. While they have been sometimes strapped for funds, the eviction is not a matter of rent payment, but rather the fact that the landlord has decided he wants the unit for himself. In an apartment complex where there are only a few units and where the landlord already lives, this can be legal. While inconvenienced, neither Bob nor Adele seems terribly put out by the fact that they will have to move. In fact, Bob's overall affect is one of stoicism, an unusual trait in an artist. Bob paints scenes of wildlife and landscapes as a hobby. They hang on the walls of their home. Bob explains that finding out that he had AIDS was devastating. Adele says that Bob would later characterize it by saying that those initial days after diagnosis were days where each moment was just like the feeling one gets during an earthquake. "It rattles you for a second, and then your heart beats wildly, but that's what it's like all day long, every time you think about it."

The Christmas when Bob was diagnosed with AIDS proved to be only the beginning of more heartache. The man Bob says he was "with" was his lover, Greg. Not long after Bob's diagnosis, Greg also fell ill and was given a diagnosis of AIDS. But Greg's health decline was dramatic, and while Bob took care of him, he was also holding down his job, which carried with it a great deal of responsibility. "His case was much more advanced than mine," says Bob.

It seemed ironic to Bob that while he was diagnosed first, Greg was going downhill so fast. Greg suffered from lymphoma, toxoplasmosis, and a host of opportunistic infections to which people with AIDS are vulnerable. To Bob, the spectacle of what was happening to Greg was like an omen, a crystal ball into which he could peer at his own future, full of illness and suffering. "I was hooking him up to IVs and watching him dwindle away, knowing that I had the same thing in me.

"The doctor kept telling me that my case wasn't as severe as Greg's, but to watch your fate right next to you is hard. I would leave the house for work after hooking him up to an IV and drive to work praying that everything would go ok. Meanwhile, when I got to work, I had to pretend that everything was rosy."

The pressure of taking care of Greg, perceiving his own future in Greg's present, and keeping everything a secret seemed to harden Bob's already natural tendency to keep quiet into a wall of denial about his life that was seemingly impenetrable.

Adele helped Bob overcome that tendency. She became his best friend. "I knew everything that was going on in his relationship. Absolutely everything. I saw the whole ball of wax that was involved in taking care of Greg," she says.

Their friendship continued during the decline of Greg's health and through the mounting pressures Bob was under both at work and at home. Bob's own health began to fail. "Once I was put on the medication, it really messed with my system," he explains. "You are finding out that your body is suddenly working differently and you can't gain weight." Bob began to lose weight without gaining it back, and he had trouble sleeping. His eyes were rimmed with red, his hair lost its luster, and he was haggard.

His condition did not go unnoticed at work. "It's a very conservative company," he explains, "and a single guy that's with the company a long time and who isn't married gets the attention of the executives." Bob mentions that there were many approaches made by different women at the various hotel sites he had worked. "And when I didn't seem to respond, I guess they started building their own thoughts."

"People were speculating," says Adele. "Some people," she adds, "are very comfortable with themselves, and others who aren't need to speculate about the sexuality of others."

"There was some push for me to change jobs," says Bob.

"It was a squeeze," says Adele.

"I was approached," says Bob.

"They gave him an ultimatum," says Adele.

"During a hotel opening, the corporate director asked me to meet with him. At the meeting he asked me about my sexual preference. I didn't confirm or deny anything either way, because I didn't think it had any relevance at all." Bob relates the scene of the meeting, saying that it was implied that the only reason he was in a management position was because the person who had arranged it was also gay. After the meeting, Bob's job was eliminated, and he was transferred to the food and beverage division, into a much more grueling and physically rigorous job. Later, Adele asserts that his old position was resurrected with a new title, and a different person was brought in.

Bob states that he didn't at any time consider trying to pursue any charges of discrimination. Things happened so quickly, during a period of time when his health was declining and Greg was very sick, that he did not consider it.

In addition to the added responsibilities, Bob had to take a cut in pay. The schedule was relentless and coincided with Bob's taking a turn for the worse. "They worked me 12-hour days, back to back," he says. "I would go in at six in the morning and then go home at ten o'clock at night and then go back the next day at six in the morning. My system just wasn't adjusting, my eyes were constantly bloodshot, with bags under my eyes. People were always asking me why my eyes were so red."

Bob acknowledges that the human resources department of the corporation had knowledge of his HIV condition by virtue of the fact that he had made claims on his medical insurance, but he doesn't believe that the person in charge of those claims would have breached his confidentiality to anyone else within the company. Whether or not that happened, Bob did not have his old job, he had less pay, and he had to perform physically demanding work for longer hours than before. In fact, he would have had grounds for a case of discrimination, but the case would not have been an easy one. It is a distinct possibility that his company would not have yielded at the threat of a lawsuit, and the long involvement and energy that it might have required did not appear to be something Bob could emotionally or physically and perhaps even psychologically afford at the time.

Bob tried his best to keep up appearances not only at the new job but at the doctor's as well. He had it in his head that if everything *looked* all right, then it *was* all right. "I visited Greg several times while he was in the hospital," says Bob. "He would tell me about his fear. After that, I became afraid of any of the tests, or when the doctor recommended I should get x-rayed, I would always tense out. I couldn't imagine going through any of those series of events that Greg went through. So I just tried to steer clear of that stuff by making myself appear healthier and tell the doctor that everything was fine."

Basically, in Bob's mind, if the doctor wrote down that Bob weighed more, then he weighed more. If Bob didn't complain that he was short of breath, then he wasn't. "I guess," he says, "that if I didn't hear myself complain, or if I tried to remove myself from it, rather than go to the doctor and point out every little thing that was wrong with me, I would pretend I didn't feel bad. I guess I thought by talking about it or hearing myself say it, I would somehow be weaker."

On days when he went to the doctor, Bob would prepare the fictional Bob for the examination. Since one of the routine things the doctor would do was to ask him about his energy and weigh him, Bob would eat huge pasta meals the night before: "The day before my doctor's appointment, I would always eat a lot, and drink lots of water, whatever I could do before going in. I would always say to the doctor that I was fine, and basically, in comparison to what Greg went through, I was fine."

Before stepping into the doctor's office, Bob would go to great lengths to deceive both the doctor and himself. He drank the water to make himself weigh more. He would place weights in the pockets of his clothes to add pounds. Adele admits to her complicity in the situation. "I was one of the ones who helped him by feeding him before he went to the doctor. I didn't understand it either, but it was important to Bob."

Eventually, the strain of the job became too much for Bob. He finally acknowledged that he had to go out on disability. "I was drenched under my suits at work and becoming very skeletal," remembers Bob. "I wasn't looking good or feeling good or sleeping or eating. I wouldn't have lasted. I made the judgment call myself, but I don't feel that I would have lasted."

Before going out on disability, at the urging of his physician Bob had contacted the local AIDS service organization about becoming a client. The doctor thought Bob would need help wading through his insurance issues. He got the application papers for the organization and then put them on top of his refrigerator, leaving them there for a time. "It was that denial thing," says Adele. "He didn't want any part of it at first."

"Yeah," says Bob, smiling, "I played with that application for a while."

"A very long time, remember? It ping-ponged back and forth. You didn't want to be part of the organization because Greg had used it too." Bob nods.

Eventually, however, he gathered the paperwork together and sent it in so that he could get help. After an intake and assessment, Bob got counseling on how to apply for disability, which he then did and left work.

"Where he was and what he looked like then compared to what he is now is almost as if it is two different people," says Adele. "The person he was before, his hair was unhealthy, his skin was uneven, there was stress in his life and you saw it. But now, his whole demeanor, the body, the skin, the eyes are clear, there are no sores in his mouth and his hair looks great."

Bob agrees. "Once I went onto disability, I didn't have such a problem with not sleeping and losing weight. My weight stabilized and I slept better. My eyes weren't so red anymore."

It would have been ideal if Bob's troubles had ended with his leaving work and enjoying a return to relative health. But it wasn't as easy as that. He was soon to discover that the denial that caused him to put weights into his pockets and put on the false face for his doctor had a price.

"I went onto state disability for a year, and during that time I made my application for long-term disability," explains Bob.

Bob was much sicker than he had ever let on and sicker than he ever wanted to admit. Not only was he having the physical symptomology he ignored or didn't talk about, his immune system was seriously damaged. AIDS is a condition that comes about as a result of the depletion of the immune system. One indicator of the health of the immune system, most simply stated, is the number of t cells one has. A healthy person generally has between 800 and 1200 T cells. The CDC classifies a person as having AIDS when the T cell level falls below 200. When Bob was diagnosed with his painful thrush in 1991, and when he left work to go out on disability, he had just 4 T cells.

The next shock for Bob, however, was when his claim for long-term disability was denied by the insurance company. After viewing his medical records and work history, the company determined that Bob, with his devastated immune system, was too healthy for disability. For one brief month upon his leaving employment and going out on state disability, Bob's T cell level spiked to 80, but the following month it fell back to his floor of 4.

Bob's first reaction was typical for him. "At first I just put it out of my head and tried to figure out what I was going to do. I thought I should try to go back to work. I had to figure things out."

The denial of disability coverage was confounding to Bob. "I'd been with the company for 10 years. I don't understand that. They said I wasn't sick enough." It was difficult for Bob to accept, but the fact that he had been a good employee had nothing whatever to do with the business decisions of his employer's insurance company.

Bob's medical records, he says, were somewhat vague. There were references to bouts of pain but no real signs of distress other than his extraordinarily low T cell counts. There were also the prescriptions. At the time Bob made his disability claim, he was taking AZT, DDI, Bactrim, Imodium, Darvitol, Zovirax, and Micalbutin, among others. Later, the list would grow.

After the shock of the denial wore off, Bob went for help to the AIDS service organization he had been reluctant to seek out. There he was assisted in filing an appeal, which is now pending.

The past few years have been tumultuous for Bob. He was successful in a high-level job. He was involved in a relationship. Suddenly, with the appearance one day of a sore throat, his world came to a halt and was turned completely upside down. He was diagnosed and at the same time became caretaker to his companion, who eventually died. He faced his own illness and subsequent trouble at work. He found that he could no longer work and was denied disability in spite of his completely depleted immune system.

This would be a lonely experience. Most people could not understand what Bob was going through. By good fortune, Bob's family was very supportive. He told them in 1992. "It was hard," he says, "but they handled it very well, and my mother, when I had told her about the thrush that I had the previous Christmas, she rushed to a medical journal and so she had pretty much figured it out." Bob's three sisters and two brothers also know, and with the exception of his oldest sister, who Bob says could not deal with the issues, they have been supportive.

Bob also had the support of friends, most obviously Adele. Adele had listened to Bob when he needed to talk, about his diagnosis, about Greg, about his fears. One evening in 1992, while they were working together at a New Year's party, they made a confession to one another about the depth to which they cared. In February of 1993, they began to live together. "It all happened very nicely," says Adele, "very romantically. It was tough, though, very tough."

While living together, they came to terms with the next step. On July 4, Independence Day, a day purposely chosen for its significance, Bob and Adele eloped to Las Vegas and got married, the last couple to be married before midnight. "I had never lived with anyone before," explains Adele, "but I always knew I'd marry the man I lived with. It just seemed like a logical step."

Admittedly, it was a big step. "We drove to Las Vegas," says Adele, smiling. "That was an even bigger test of will, with a four and a half hour drive to analyze one another and our motives. There was lots of time to turn around."

Adele knows that this is not the conventional way people get married. But it makes sense to each of them. She explains, "There is no competition between us, there are no hints of the green-eyed monster. I was thirty years old when I got married. I waited a long time to make a decision about somebody," she says.

Rather than being shocked, their friends have offered support. "Many of my friends who now know my situation and know Bob fall in love with Bob," says Adele. "They also know what is happening in our lives. There have just been so many people reaching out to help. We've had a very high level of support for what we are doing and what we are going through." She acknowledges that the situation is not ordinary. "But people who have known me for a long time know I wouldn't have gotten into this unless I really loved this man. I went into this with my eyes open."

When the insurance company turned Bob down, the appeal was filed. As part of the appeal, Adele wrote a letter, which was as follows:

> I met my husband in January 1991. We were part of an opening team for a five star resort. We befriended one another and soon established a bond. Bob confided in me when he was diagnosed with AIDS. It was an unforgettable time for me. I was the first one he had confided in outside of his family. I knew immediately what my purpose was: I was to be by his side every step of the way through this potentially difficult ordeal. I love my husband as a man and like him as my best friend. We were married on July 4, 1994. We eloped, much to the surprise of both our parents.
>
> Bob shared all his doctor's results with me. He lived from appointment to appointment. The numerical results were the culprits. And it was these medical and numerical results that we would defy. Bob was in a state of denial; he could not believe that his life was in such a state of decay. Bob stated to me on several occasions how fearful he was. Bob was afraid of the permanent information that his medical record would contain regarding his disease. Bob, on various reports, was uncomfortable with the lack of concern expressed by his doctor. The level of time that the doctor spent with Bob was very minimal—especially because Bob had to wait four to six week intervals before the doctor had time to see him. It was the medical staff that spent a fraction more time with Bob during his medical appointments.
>
> Bob's intention was deliberate—to create medical results contrary to how he really felt. So we began. Prior to each doctor's appointment, Bob would bulk up on protein drinks, eat masses of carbohydrates (pasta, oatmeal, cereals, and so on). He would keep weights and lead tape with him when weighed. I soon became involved even further at home. Between B12 shots and foraging and binging at home we kept his weight up. Bob had chefs at work making him pastries and full-course meals for breakfast, lunch, and sometimes dinner. All this in preparation for his appointment with his doctor.

Bob had only 4 T cells. He was adding to his list of medications with every appointment. He was fearful.

Bob was indirectly forced to change jobs within the company after he was approached by the corporate director of human resources regarding his alleged sexual preference. Bob had to take a different position. It was not a lateral move. The position he held before was a management position, between 40 and 50 hours a week. The job he stepped into turned disastrous. The new job involved 16-hour work days, six days a week. He had doubled his work week, to 96 hours from 50 hours before.

Bob was not doing well. He was thin and drawn. Fellow employees would come to me and ask me what was wrong with Bob. His eyes were red all the time. He never smiled; he was a walking skeleton. He had difficulty with his sight, suffering pain from headaches. His night sweats were more prevalent. The outbreaks of topical lip blisters were camouflaged as best he could with Zovirax. He went into work without complaint—with bloodshot eyes, aches from within his joints, pain in his head—to fear of what would happen to him next. We hid it at work also. Nobody could know or suspect he was sick. So against better judgment, he stayed the very long work hours, longer weeks, suffering silently.

Bob also felt a new set of pressures, aside from daily living. He would torment himself with questions. "Could I keep up the perception people had of my image alive at work, with my parents, with Adele's parents?" "What would anybody think if I quit working?" So Bob stayed longer than he ever should with the company and with this guise that all was well. It was very painful for me to see him try to make it up and out into the world, knowing what I knew as a wife and a friend.

Bob has had to stumble through life currently thinking like a 60-year-old man at the age of 33 years. Bob tries to keep his mind exercised with the idea of hope. For Bob to think about applying for state disability, social security, and then long-term disability in hopes of survival is maddening to him.

Bob and I have lost both our own cars; I've pawned wedding gifts; creditors call constantly. Sentimental jewelry that has been in our family for years had to be sold. We have lost it all.

Nothing is more important than the respect that I have for the willpower to live. And living is something that has not been taken from us. Our dignity we will never sacrifice.

In hindsight, perhaps Bob should have let the cards fall where they may with regard to work. However, until you have felt the wrath of hell pulling on you daily, that at any time you could die, or be scrutinized as an AIDS patient, you could not understand this heartfelt sentiment.

Adele poignantly outlines Bob's story of denial. Bob has less reason to be in denial these days. Though things have been rough, he has not been alone. The bittersweet experience that any life-threatening situation presents is that there is often the possibility of bringing people closer together and adding a new level of appreciation for even the smallest things. That, perhaps, is one of the many clichés that AIDS brings to life. Bob and Adele found each other, something that, had there been no such thing as AIDS, might never have happened. Now, things have changed.

"We don't do those things anymore," notes Adele. "I mean now when we see the doctor, it is always a very positive experience. We don't even think about T cells anymore. It's not part of our subject matter. It's just eating well and surviving one day at a time."

Bob admits there is no more denial. "I try to forget about AIDS as much as I can, but I've also come to terms with it," he says. "If I had it to do over again, I would have faced what I was up against sooner. I would have gone to the doctor to see the seriousness of it and stopped to think about where life is going and I would have tried not to waste any day."

Bob's story is one of denial, but it shows how denial can be pierced and replaced by something else, some other incentive. It is also an excellent example of how, within the context of one illness over a period of a few years, a single person can encounter several legal predicaments. Bob probably suffered discrimination for being gay and for having AIDS on the job. He is facing a legal eviction. And he has insurance issues that may have a dramatic impact on his well-being.

Bob goes to a different doctor now, one he feels more comfortable with. All in all, Bob is much more comfortable with life. During the time she helped Bob load up on carbohydrates and food before he went to the doctor, Adele referred to AIDS in her journal as the dark shadow in their lives. She didn't want to give it the name AIDS because that would give it too much power over their lives. The shadow of AIDS sits on Bob's shoulder still, but there has been a sea change in his relationship with his dark phantom. "It is still like a ball and chain," he says, "but now I am dragging it along—it's not pulling me or holding me back anymore."

8

Hear No Evil, Speak No Evil
Testing and Confidentiality

Whatsoever I shall see or hear in the course of my
profession in my intercourse with men, if it be what
should not be published abroad, I will never divulge,
holding such things to be holy secrets.

Hippocrates

The notion of patient confidentiality in medical treatment is not a new concept. In fact, it is a long-established medical tradition that the relationship between a provider of health care and his or her patient is a protected one. The reasoning behind this practice is based on the belief that if a patient cannot honestly confide in his or her physician about intimate subjects, then he or she is apt to go untreated. The nature of the patient's relationship to the physician must be held sacred by the rest of society.

Treatment matters are not the only aspect of medical care that the patient may prefer to keep confidential. The very fact that one is ill is personal. As noted in Chapter 5, discrimination is based on the perception of stigma. In turn, stigma has historically been linked with disease. Throughout the ages, epidemics in particular have drawn stigma. They have been perceived as scourges of God punishing the sinner. In the earliest days of the United States, when a ship in a colonial harbor had come from an area of plague or epidemic, a day of fasting might be declared in order to appease God, who used illness to punish sin. Smallpox, yellow fever, and plague were all deemed at one time or another to have resulted from the judgment of God. At the turn of the century, syphilitic prostitutes were treated terribly. As recently as mid-twentieth century America, many considered cancer to be a source of shame.

Manifestations of this sentiment are common in a world where AIDS exists. In Nairobi, Kenya, for example, a Catholic priest announced that he would refuse to conduct funeral services for people who died of AIDS, saying that if he were to do so, "The church might be seen to be encouraging the spread of the disease." In modern-day America, even with the levels of knowledge of science and virology that society now has, there are still those who would equate the HIV epidemic with divine punishment, as was seen when the Reverend Billy Graham stated in 1993 his belief that the AIDS epidemic might be a judgment of God, a statement he recanted afterwards. But especially because AIDS is transmitted by means of sexual intercourse, and in America, most often by homosexual intercourse, a practice deemed outside of morality by many, the equation of sex to punishment will stand. Graham himself, in making his statement in Cleveland, Ohio, rationalized it by saying that God intended sex to be in the context of marriage only. This powerful combination of illness and morality works to create an extremely potent stigma.

Stigma—the act of making someone different, of making an "other" out of a fellow human being—satisfies a vast array of needs for those who don't belong to the "other." This function is the very basis for discrimination (see Chapter 4). Acts of discrimination are one effect of stigma, while policies borne out of the creation of an "other" is another. There is an "other" if your skin is a different color; there is an "other" if you speak a different language or worship differently. Some legal theorists, as David Schulman noted in Chapter 5, find a basis for stigma in the way certain people might be perceived to be "polluting" on some level. That one is ill with disease appears to be yet another manifestation of "pollution" and therefore is a basis for stigma. The need to create stigma and cast some in the role of "other" begins with the majority's need to feel safe and secure from the perceived inroads of a minority. It is not this simple, though. The urge to stigmatize comes from a complicated variety of psychological and sociological causes that are beyond the scope of this, or perhaps any, book. But the fact is that it exists and we see it every day.

Given the issues rising from the stigma of disease, particularly with respect to people with HIV and those perceived to be at risk for HIV, the issue of confidentiality becomes one of paramount importance. No other disease in history has had the stigma attached to it that HIV disease has had, making confidentiality important not only for those affected, but for our entire public health-care system. As long as the powerful stigma is present, HIV medical treatment has to be confidential.

BACKGROUND—HIV EXCEPTIONALISM

With HIV disease, the combination of sex and drugs, transmission and mortality has heightened the air of blame that has often accompanied the experience of falling ill. The populations most affected by AIDS—gays, persons of color, and women—were already perceived as "other" in some capacity. Now, having HIV or being in a class of persons with a higher incidence of HIV burdens them with another layer of "other." A gay person of color who was tested positive for HIV has layer upon layer of circumstances that will, in the eyes of many, make him "other" and therefore subject to all kinds of discrimination.

Many public health experts feel that, in spite of stigma, HIV should be treated like any other illness or epidemic, often citing past victories or near-victories over diseases like syphilis or other sexually transmitted diseases. That model is based on finding those infected, identifying their contacts, and, meanwhile, intervening with education to prevent further infections and to cure.

But with HIV, the model breaks down at an obvious juncture. There is, as yet, no cure. And the weight of stigma is greater than that which accompanies other sexually transmitted diseases.

Elizabeth Cooper, a public interest lawyer and professor at Brooklyn Law School, points to the flood of litigation that exists around HIV discrimination. "If you look to the numbers of discrimination cases that surround syphilis," she says, "and compare them to the numbers of cases involving HIV, there is just no comparison. With syphilis there are a few cases each year, while with HIV, there are hundreds."

Early in the epidemic, a public health doctrine evolved that divorced HIV from the traditional model for handling sexually transmitted disease. The doctrine is known as "HIV exceptionalism," a term first coined by Ronald Bayer in the *New England Journal of Medicine*.

HIV exceptionalism is a reaction to the stigma of HIV and to the fact that the traditional model for sexually transmitted disease care does not work. It originated in the need to create an environment in which people could come forward for testing and feel somewhat safe. If stigma made testing unsafe, it was reasoned, HIV exceptionalism and the construction of laws of confidentiality could make it safe. The stigma could not be eliminated, but the effects of it could be deterred.

State legislatures around the nation, particularly in the epicenters of the AIDS epidemic, enacted laws providing for the confidentiality of people who stepped forward to take an HIV-antibody test. It became illegal in many jurisdictions to reveal to third parties that a person had tested antibody-positive. In addition, as noted in Chapter 5, antidiscrimination legislation was also advanced, protecting people against discrimination as a result of being HIV-positive.

The entire construct of law, therefore, was in support of public health. The objective was to maintain a safe environment for people to be tested. If more people felt safe in coming forward for voluntary testing, then people who were infected would discover their status at an early stage of the HIV disease, preventing unknowing transmission to other parties. "When you assure an individual that his or her rights to privacy and confidentiality will be protected," says Liz Cooper, "you create a much more hospitable environment for someone to come in and take a risk and be tested."

Therefore, the entire public health strategy to beat the AIDS epidemic has been based on a new model, one that was an exception to the established rule for sexually transmitted diseases.

Cooper espouses the philosophy that public health principles and civil rights protections work in hand, not against one another: "When people portray issues around HIV as being protective of the public health versus protective of the civil rights of the individual, it is very upsetting. In fact, by protecting one, you automatically protect the other."

Some people have argued that HIV exceptionalism contributes to the stigma of HIV by treating AIDS as something special. According to this argument, by virtue of the fact that we treat it differently by law, people will treat people with HIV differently, reinforcing the stigma by recognizing it. It is a sort of chicken or egg proposition. But Cooper maintains that while she believes "that there is some limited value to the notion that the more we treat people differently, the more they will be different, I also believe that if we don't respect and understand and acknowledge the stigma and discrimination that persists with AIDS, then we are going to develop bad and hurtful policies."

TESTING TODAY

"HIV has shown us all of the cracks and flaws in our society," says Liz Cooper. "It is like injecting a dye and seeing where all of the cracks have occurred. AIDS has been a call to consciousness to see how badly our system and our safety net works and how unfairly people treat one another." The vortex for all treatment of people with AIDS, good or bad, is the HIV-antibody test. In the entire course of the epidemic, it is the only solid tool that we have developed against the virus. It is the means by which one becomes aware of one's status and gains medical treatment. Sadly, it is also the means by which discrimination and maltreatment by others occurs.

Given this reality, deciding when and where to take an HIV test is a very personal decision, fraught with more complications than meet the eye. As a result of media misinformation, most people assume, in fact, that the test is for AIDS, but it is not. The media did the general public a disservice in the mid-1980s, when the HIV antibody test was developed, by calling it the "AIDS test." Despite repeated attempts on the part of AIDS community-based organizations to educate the media in this regard, the media proved singularly uneducable. The "AIDS test" is not a test for AIDS, but rather, a test for the presence of the antibody that your system has developed in response to Human Immunodeficiency Virus. The difference is more than technical.

Having the antibody generally would mean that you harbor the virus, though not always, as seen with newborns. A test can prove false positive or false negative. A newborn might be tested and show HIV-positive, when in fact the test is revealing the presence of the mother's antibodies, not the baby's. The baby may not have the virus at all. A negative test, in and of itself, is not proof that one does not harbor the virus. There is a window period of time after the virus is introduced into the human system before the body reacts with the formation of its own antibody to the virus. The length of that period may vary for individuals. During the 1993 International AIDS Conference in Berlin, there was a great deal of discussion concerning people who tested HIV-negative up until the time of their diagnosis.

A person should know as much as possible about an HIV test before taking it. It will prove to be more than a test of the immune system. An HIV-antibody test does not occur in a medical vacuum. It is a test of your insurability, of your friends, of your family, of your relationship with a spouse or significant other, of your employer, of your legal rights, and of your physician's loyalty to you. Most of all, it tests your own ability to cope with circumstances that may be very difficult to face. An HIV-antibody test puts every system in your life on the line. Before taking the test, you should be sure that the circumstances in your life are ideal for doing so. If you are thinking of switching jobs, it may be best to wait until you clear the preexisting condition term of a new insurance contract (see Chapter 6). Deciding when and where to be tested is, therefore, extremely important.

In 1993, the *American Journal of Public Health* reported on a 1990 study by Ronald O. Valdiserri on American knowledge levels about testing availability. The researchers conducted a random-digit telephone survey that spanned 44 states in addition to the District of Columbia. Two-thirds of the 81,557 respondents stated that the place to go for an HIV test was to a physician, while only 14 percent named public sites and 12 percent said that they did not know where to go for testing. There is little, if any, reason to believe that awareness in this regard has changed at all.

This survey is telling on a number of accounts. First and foremost, it would appear that most Americans would go for testing to a venue where they would receive little or no counseling regarding their HIV status. Secondly, it reveals that there is little perception of the different ways to be tested in the United States.

Early in the epidemic, when there were few options, many people went for an HIV test by donating blood. This was not a very desirable method, if for no other reasons than that it placed a strain on the blood banks and that there was no pretest or posttest counseling.

There are basically three types of testing. The first, anonymous testing, is available in most states. Anonymous testing occurs at specifically designated sites. You go in for a blood test and your identity remains unknown throughout your entire transaction, even should you test positive. You are identified only by a number. In a week or two, you can go back and get the results of your test, usually, and in the best circumstances, accompanied by good quality face-to-face counseling. Anonymous testing offers many advantages. First and foremost, and most obvious, your identity is not revealed and no one has your name to share with an employer, a physician, a parent, a teacher, or, most important of all, an insurance company. Secondly, from society's point of view, anonymous testing sites attract the greatest number of persons who are likely to be HIV-positive. Thirdly, it would appear that the rate of testing generally increases when testing is offered anonymously. In southern Ontario, the rate of testing more than doubled when anonymous testing was introduced, indicating that anonymity may double the requests for testing. Lastly, at an anonymous test site, counseling is available.

There is a big difference between *anonymous testing* and *confidential testing*. The settings for confidential testing may vary. One might be a clinic specializing in the treatment of sexually transmitted diseases. It could be a community health center or special site set up solely for the purpose of providing an HIV test. Or, the setting could be your doctor's office. In some circumstances, if you are applying for a life insurance policy, it could even be at the behest of a life insurance company. It is important to remember, however, that whoever is testing you, confidential testing is not anonymous. The tester knows your name but promises not to reveal the results of your test to anyone. Confidential testing may, but does not always, involve counseling. There are exceptions to that rule that we will get to later.

The third way to be tested is without your consent or knowledge. Despite safeguards and laws that are designed to protect a person, this abuse nevertheless occurs. There are laws against murder, too, but it still happens. One should not suppose that testing will not occur simply because permission was not asked to perform a test. In Illinois, in 1994, a physician tested her patient for HIV over his own objections to being tested and then revealed the fact that the patient was HIV-positive to his sexual partner. In Maryland, a man sued the state because he was forced by officials to take an HIV test based on their belief that he was knowingly spreading HIV.

There may, in the near future, be a fourth way to be tested. Biotechnical companies are spawning new methods of testing. A company named Epitope in Oregon was granted Food and Drug Administration (FDA) approval for a new test called OraSure, which tests saliva for HIV-antibodies. Far less expensive than a blood test, this method offers physicians and community clinics an option in testing that will result in further ethical dilemmas as well as a widening potential for abuse. It should be noted that, for now, the test may only be used in a physician's office.

In addition, Johnson and Johnson has developed a home HIV test kit that the company claims is as reliable as other testing methods. This method permits anonymous testing in the home but has not yet been approved by the FDA. The date of its arrival on the market therefore depends on that agency. To test, you would buy a kit at a pharmacy, much in the way that people can now buy a home pregnancy or cholesterol test kit. You draw a few drops of blood with a finger prick and then put them on blotting paper. You send this paper to the Johnson and Johnson laboratory for testing. You then telephone for your results and are connected to someone for counseling and referral if your test is HIV-positive. Critics of this method, particularly lesbian and gay health clinics, charge that there must be face-to-face counseling for it to be effective and that this testing method runs serious risk of increasing suicide by HIV-positive persons. The fact is, however, that there is currently no quality standard for face-to-face counseling set by the Centers for Disease Control, and there are no studies indicating that face-to-face counseling will be any more or less effective than a telephone counselor. According to the Centers for Disease Control in 1995, most Americans take an HIV test with private physicians, who are less likely to offer counseling. In fact, the CDC discovered that approximately one-third of people tested did so in a publicly funded clinic, such as a confidential or anonymous test site. In comparing the two, the CDC found that an average of 60.7 percent of those people who took the test at a public clinic received counseling compared to only 28.2 percent who received counseling at private sites. Physicians for the most part are not discussing any HIV issues with patients, as demonstrated by a 1993 study that showed that only 20 percent of physicians even discussed HIV with their patients. This is despite a widely felt yearning by patients.* Therefore, the advantage to "home

*In 1995, Harvard Medical School released a survey of Boston high school students that revealed that 85 percent wanted their doctors to give them information about HIV but only 27 percent had ever had such a discussion with their physicians. While 70 percent stated that they wanted to discuss safer sexual practices with their doctors, 70 percent also stated that they would not feel comfortable bringing up the subject themselves.

collection" testing is that it will open up anonymous HIV testing to millions of people who otherwise would not avail themselves of a test at all, who prefer testing in a confidential setting to an anonymous setting, or who might go to a physician for a test, but receive no counseling. Home collection kits under consideration by the FDA include a component of counseling by telephone when receiving HIV-positive test results.

Undoubtedly, methods of testing will continue to advance scientifically. Varied types of collection kits for use in home and the physician's office will be offered, making testing easier to access. However, with advanced testing technology comes advanced potential for abuse in testing, particularly with respect to the testing of a person without consent or knowledge. For example, kits offering the home collection of a blood sample or the more readily available saliva may open the way for surreptitious testing by a third party. A foster parent might test a foster child without the child's consent or knowledge, or an employer may tell an applicant that in order to apply for a job, he or she must supply a blood sample. The fact that the act is illegal does not mean that it won't happen. Be cautious with the new methodologies offered in testing. It is extremely important to share knowledge of your test in ways only you choose.

The primary difference between methods of testing that offer anonymous and confidential testing, other than the obvious fact that in the former you are not known and in the latter you are, is the fact that with anonymous testing *you* are solely in control of the results of your test. In the confidential setting, you are not in control; you share that control with your doctor and anyone else who has access to your medical records, now or in the future. This is not to imply that confidential testing is not as good as anonymous, but that with respect to the control of your test results, you have the optimum amount of control with the anonymous setting.

The circumstances for taking an HIV-antibody test should be of one's own choosing and not at the urging of another, be it a partner, a parent, a physician, or employer. Taking an HIV-antibody test is not like taking any other kind of medical test. It does not occur in a medical vacuum. It is a test of everything you may value.

Simply put, take the test when you think it is best to take it, not when someone else thinks so.

Equally important, choose carefully with whom you share your test results and when. This is something over which you should be in control, not someone else. Community-based AIDS service organizations have long recommended that people choose anonymous test sites when and where available. Despite that, most people test in a physician's office. That decision is a fine one, and within your control, but in doing so, bear in mind that you are also sharing your test results with the medical staff at your physician's office. Moreover, it has not been unheard of that, upon finding a patient is HIV-positive, physicians have refused to treat him or her or have attempted to refer the patient elsewhere (see Chapter 9). The information is of such a nature that you should be in control of dispensing it when and where you want and need to under the appropriate circumstances. The beginning of most HIV/AIDS discrimination is when the information about antibody status is given to people who, for one reason or another, can't handle it.

As stated earlier, an important component of any testing program involves good counseling and referral, though even at government funded confidential test sites and anonymous test sites counselors are not always available to help a person cope with the news of an HIV test, whether positive or negative. Counseling should include safer sex and needle-sharing guidelines, and information on how to avoid infection, or, if already infected with HIV, reinfection. Counseling should also include referral to the various types of services one might need. Counseling is a component of the home collection kits that are under development. A consequence of choosing to test in a physician's office, however, may be that counseling is not made available to you. If the physician is one with whom you do not have an established relationship, then you run the further risk of getting very upsetting news delivered in an offensive or blunt manner. Consider the circumstance of taking a test in a physician's office carefully, and plan it out.

Another note with respect to taking an HIV test in a physician's office: many women report that they inquire about an HIV test with their gynecologist and are turned down, being told that they are not at risk. This seems particularly true for Caucasian women who are perceived to be at low risk by the physician. A physician's refusal to test diminishes the partnership quality of your care, but it also puts you at medical risk should you feel that you may have been exposed to HIV. If this happens, change gynecologists.

Before taking an HIV test, take into account the following considerations:

- Are you emotionally ready to hear the news, whether the results are positive or negative?
- Are you ready to discuss the results with your sexual partners?
- Are you in a stable job environment and covered by your insurance plan?
- If you have an individual policy for insurance, has your preexisting period of coverage passed (see Chapter 6)?
- Have you considered all testing options, that is, confidential testing sites, anonymous testing sites, your physician's office, or, if available, home collection testing?
- Have you telephoned a local AIDS service organization or AIDS hotline for advice?

If you decide to take the test with your physician, consider the following:

- Choose a physician with whom you are comfortable.
- Share with the physician any concerns you may have about confidentiality, particularly regarding insurance.
- Ask if counseling and referral is available.
- Find out if your physician treats HIV, or if he or she will send you elsewhere for treatment.

Exceptions to Confidentiality

As outlined above, because the ramifications of taking an HIV test are so vast and because there was the potential for so much abuse, legislators in high HIV-incidence states passed confidentiality legislation, prohibiting the disclosure of HIV test results to unauthorized persons.

However, with the enactment of confidentiality legislation, it became apparent that there needed to be exceptions to strict confidentiality. Medical personnel, for instance, need to exchange medical information about the patient in the course of treatment. Other circumstances have caused a tempering of the confidentiality statutes that were enacted early in the epidemic.

Today, many people argue that there are enough safeguards protecting people with AIDS against unfair treatment and discrimination, so confidentiality restrictions on HIV should be diminished or dissolved altogether in the interest of learning more about the epidemic and the people who are infected.

The earliest legislation in New York and California was fairly stringent, making it difficult, it was argued, for medical personnel to do their jobs. Confidentiality statutes were thereafter modified to allow medical personnel to exchange medical information that would include HIV status. Liz Cooper cites the fact that early in the epidemic people were afraid and that that fear motivated tough statutes: "People were afraid that this disease might ultimately affect them or their children and they were willing to be more protective than they might otherwise be." In addition, because AIDS was such an unknown factor, legislators tended to defer to physicians and their expertise in their recommendations.

However, there was a situation that caught public attention and became a lightning rod for moral indignation at the AIDS epidemic—the knowing and intentional infection of another person with HIV. This resulted not only in calls for the criminalization of HIV transmission but for a weakening of confidentiality statutes and the doctrine of HIV exceptionalism. One man in New York relayed a story of dating a woman for a three-month period, during which they had an active sex life. Suddenly, after three months, his partner called off the relationship. Her parting words were to tell him that he had better get tested for HIV because she had AIDS and she was determined to take as many men with her as she could.

Just three days before that, the man had donated blood for his father's heart bypass surgery. An HIV-antibody test on that blood might be inconclusive, given the fact that there is a period of six weeks to six months before the body develops antibodies that will be detected in an HIV test. The man had very little recourse.

Because of the intentional transmission of HIV by some, confidentiality statutes were amended once again. Legislators wanted to address the fact that someone might be posing a threat and that the physician might be able to stop him or her. An exception to confidentiality was added to many confidentiality statutes to allow a physician to inform a third party of the impending danger posed by his patient if the doctor believed that the patient was not going to comply with safer needle-sharing or sex practices.

The physician is in an extremely unenviable situation. Take, for example, the case of a physician who has a homosexual client who is deeply closeted, HIV-positive, and married. The physician counsels the patient on safer sexual practices and the patient explains that his wife is determined to have children and that therefore condoms are out of the question. Also out of the question is telling his wife about his true lifestyle. What is the physician to do?

Under most of the modified confidentiality statutes, a physician *may* inform the third party who is at risk but is not necessarily under an obligation to do so. Some statutes, as in New York and California, give the physician the option of informing the county health department, which in turn may inform the at-risk partner.

The statutory situation is complicated further by case law not even related to HIV/AIDS. In the 1980s, a man told his therapist that he intended to kill his girlfriend, a situation about which the therapist did nothing. Unfortunately, his client did do something; he went through with his threat and murdered his girlfriend. The family of the victim then sued the therapist for his failure to stop the murder. The therapist defended himself by citing the privilege that exists between a psychiatrist and his patient. In its ruling, the court, in what is called the *Tarasoff* case, ruled against the therapist, stating that the existence of a threat to an identified third party was sufficient cause to weaken the privileged relationship of doctor–patient.

What does *Tarasoff* mean to the practicing physician who is under a statutory duty of confidentiality vis-à-vis his patient but whose patient openly states an intention not to comply with safer sexual or needle-sharing practices? The answer is not immediately clear. The law passed by the legislature may say that the physician has the option, which he may or may not exercise, to inform the third party or, at the very least, the health department. On the other hand, case law may say that if the physician knows of impending harm to a third party because of the noncompliant behavior of his patient, he may in fact be liable in a civil suit if he does not relay this information.

Mandatory Names Reporting

While statutes were enacted to protect against unlawful disclosures of HIV status, many states also enacted requirements for physicians to report the names of those found to be infected with HIV. Epidemiologists argue that such reporting helps them understand where and among whom AIDS infections are occurring. Additionally, aside from the fact that the informaton provides a better demographical understanding of the epidemic and helps target prevention campaigns to the specific populations being infected, the information also allows them to conduct contact tracing, sometimes referred to as partner notification.

Contact tracing was already an element in the model of sexually transmitted disease intervention. In the context of AIDS, it means asking the infected person to voluntarily name his or her sexual or needle-sharing partners. Those people are then contacted by health officials, informed that they have been named as an intimate contact of a person infected with HIV and offered testing and counseling services. The two advantages of mandatory names reporting—the better understanding of the flow of the virus and the ability to perform contact tracing—convinced many states to adopt a names reporting policy.

In states where there is no mandatory names reporting for HIV, only AIDS cases are reported. This presents a different picture of the epidemic to epidemiologists, being that of persons who were infected long ago and only now have compromised immune systems. Mandatory names reporting of HIV infection, however, gives a picture of the epidemic that is closer in time to the point of infection.

For the most part, states requiring mandatory names reporting have been low HIV incidence states. Recently, however, higher-incidence states, such as New Jersey, have begun to join the ranks of those requiring names reporting. Mandatory names reporting necessarily raises the question of whether or not the reporting of names has a chilling effect on people coming forward for HIV testing, counseling, and care, diminishing the safety of the testing environment.

In trying to answer the question, we must look at the populations most affected by HIV. To the greatest degree, as pointed out herein, the epidemic has impacted groups of people already disenfranchised: gay men and persons of color. The psychology and culture of these populations dictates that trust in large institutions does not reach as high a level as it may among other populations, such as white heterosexual men. In fact, large institutions have been notably oppressive to these populations. Two recent examples of this are the controversy surrounding the issue of gays in the military, where gays and lesbians have been the subject of accusations and discrimination, and California's passage of Proposition 187 in 1994. The latter is a ballot measure that states that health-care institutions shall refuse treatment to and, in fact, turn over the names of persons who are suspected of being in the country illegally. This measure turns healthcare systems into immigration systems or systems akin to the criminal justice system.

In addition to being distrustful of large institutions, these populations have felt political winds shift considerably from election to election, as noted by the success of Proposition 187 and attempts to emulate it around the nation. Consider that in California there have been ballot initiatives over the years of the AIDS epidemic that have sought quarantine of people with AIDS as well as mandatory names reporting. While those ballot initiatives ultimately failed at the polls, at the time they were presented on the ballot public opinion polls in California indicated that a majority of voters favored such measures. It was only after an expensive and extensive campaign that the measures were rejected, even in such conservative counties as Kern County in central California. In fact, the gay community had to divert time and resources from the care of people with AIDS to fight these initiatives. Given such events, why should disenfranchised populations affected by the epidemic trust the state with the names of persons who test positive for HIV? What is to be gained?

In fact, much might be lost by the presence of mandatory names reporting in high-incidence states. In studies during 1990, 60 percent of persons testing in one county in California anonymous testing sites stated that had their names been reported to the state, they would not have come in for testing. The heavy preference for privacy in testing is indicated as well in CDC studies, which demonstrate that Americans want more options for HIV testing. When asked if they intend to be tested under existing testing options, 8 percent of adults in 1992 indicated that they would seek testing in the coming year. But when asked if they would use anonymous home collection methods, the number jumped to 29 percent.

There is a very real danger that, given the psychology and culture of those affected by the epidemic, combined with the strong stigma that is still attached to having HIV infection, anonymous testing needs to be expanded and encouraged. Efforts such as mandatory names reporting stand to discourage testing by affected populations in exchange for information that is of dubious value. While contact tracing is a possible benefit, in high-incidence states the resources for contact tracing, a very labor intensive project, simply do not exist. In the final analysis, while over half the states now have mandatory names reporting, there is no evidence that the epidemic of HIV infection is under any better control in those states than in jurisdictions that do not report names.

If you are considering an HIV test and do not want your name reported to a health department, you should first inquire with your local AIDS community-based organization or your local health department whether or not HIV infection is reportable by name in your state. Remember, AIDS cases are reportable, so when you inquire, you must be clear that you are talking about HIV infection. In addition, consult Appendix E, page 224.

Mandatory Testing

In addition to exceptions to confidentiality legislation, as the epidemic continues, with little visible progress in the scientific and medical battle against the virus, calls have increased for various types of mandatory testing programs. Such a movement threatens the existence of HIV exceptionalism, a doctrine that Liz Cooper believes supports both public health and civil rights. She is opposed to any proposal that pits the rights of one sector of the population against another. But Cooper believes that frustration with the lack of progress as well as the human desire to take control over the epidemic has often led legislators to consider policies that at least give the appearance that something is being done.

"I think at this point, policy makers and the general public are sick and tired of AIDS and don't want to bothered with it any more," Cooper declares. "Therefore, they have become impatient with demands for protections and for funds. They want to make the problem go away." There is a certain appeal, she argues, to the enactment of policies that would seem to be a quick fix to the epidemic. "A very quick and easy thing for a legislator to do," she adds, "is to mandate testing in certain circumstances or to perhaps diminish confidentiality standards. Then the legislator can go home and say 'look what I've done about AIDS' and a lot of people will believe that the legislator has done something productive, when in reality that person has undermined not only civil liberties but also our public health."

Complicating any such discussion are issues that go back to the equation of disease with sin. There is sometimes a desire to enact policies that will be construed as punishing those with the disease, an exercise of morality. With the epidemic affecting primarily gay men, drug users, and persons of color, Cooper asserts, "It is easier and easier for legislators and policy makers to reinforce notions of 'other' because many people with HIV are part of communities that have traditionally been disempowered."

The entire public health strategy against AIDS, Cooper argues, has been a wise one. Strategy couched in terms of mandatory testing is not only costly but also ethically questionable. Mandatory testing programs and names reporting probably serve to drive those affected by the epidemic underground, avoiding venues where they might be tested. The result would be the further spread of AIDS by people who did not know they had it.

Proposals to institute widespread testing as a matter of routine in settings where people receive certain services have not proven to work as a measure of prevention. For instance, in 1987 Illinois passed a law requiring an HIV antibody test in order to obtain a marriage license. The result was that people went to other states for their marriage licenses; the number of licenses issued in Illinois declined by 22 percent. Routine screening in hospitals sounds logical, on its face, but in fact it would be very costly in areas where there is a low incidence of HIV. Any sort of routine, widespread testing is fraught with problems. In short, whenever a public health policy on AIDS is put forth that pits the rights of the individuals against the rights of the uninfected, it usually turns out to be a bad public health policy.

HIV antibody testing has become the focal point for almost every legal and ethical problem associated with AIDS today. Along with the discovery of the virus itself, the test and the Rock Hudson diagnosis are still the three most impacting events of the AIDS epidemic. The test was originally designed to screen blood donations to stem the flow of transmission by that route. However, with little else to help in battling the epidemic, the HIV antibody test quickly became the instrument by which many hoped to stop the spread of AIDS. Its use spread to the screening of people. Unfortunately, the test was used not solely to stop AIDS transmission but also to save money, to discriminate, and to punish and exclude people with HIV from employment, schooling, and even medical treatment.

In a society where AIDS had no stigma, the HIV test would appear to be almost perfect as a diagnostic tool. It detects the presence of antibodies to the virus and thus lets a physician know that a virus is probably present (though in the case of newborns, the antibody may actually belong to the mother; the test is merely revealing that the mother has HIV and not the child). In the case of a positive test, the physician then knows to look to immune function, monitoring T cells and immune response, prescribing antiretrovirals and, if necessary, treating opportunistic infections as they arise.

But the world of HIV testing is not ideal. Rather, the development of HIV testing and its use took place in an environment of loathing and fear of AIDS. Not only were the fatal consequences of AIDS on the minds of all Americans after the Hudson diagnosis, but the people who were most affected by AIDS at that time were gay men, injection drug users, and later, minorities—all groups who are disenfranchised from the mainstream of American culture. In fact, the environment was so poisoned with fear that AIDS community-based organizations and educators discouraged people from taking the test at all during the mid-1980s. Only after there were early medical interventions with the introduction of antiretrovirals such as AZT and DDI as well as greater protection against discrimination did such opinion leaders reconsider their position. For some, though, the environment for testing did not change enough. Without proper access to medical care, it may be argued, an HIV-antibody test does little good for the person who is infected. A test, particularly a mandatory one, seems unethical without guarantees of access to health care.

The advent of early intervention, however, speaks to the most powerful argument for mandatory testing. One can assume a degree of larger control over what is going on in the course of the disease. The decision to opt for an individual HIV-antibody test is one that says that a person wants information and knowledge in order to combat HIV personally. Both David Schulman and Liz

Cooper agree that the drive for widespread testing is often borne out of the frustration people have in experiencing such an overwhelming lack of control in the face of the epidemic.

Consequently, there have been very specific instances in which the testing of an individual without consent or knowledge is practiced as a routine matter. These examples vary greatly from state to state, though the types of mandatory testing programs are somewhat consistent.

The largest mandatory testing program is with the federal government, which tests new recruits to the armed forces. As the single largest employer in the country, the government is the biggest exception to the rule that one cannot be tested as a condition of employment. Anyone entering the armed forces is tested. The same can be said for overseas employment with the government, as with the Peace Corps.

Some criminal justice codes have provisions for the mandatory testing of persons who are convicted of a sexual offense. These provisions have a powerful emotional appeal, in that subjecting the perpetrator of a crime to HIV testing is naturally for the benefit of the crime's victim. However, such statutes encourage a false notion, that is, that one can rely on another person's HIV test. Any time one may have been exposed to HIV through unsafe sexual practices, the only reliable test is one's own. Even if a sexual criminal tests HIV antibody negative, the crime victim should rely only on his or her own test. In this regard, the existence of a statute authorizing the testing of the criminal is more for emotional satisfaction than for sound health policy.

The mandatory testing of other prisoners will also vary from state to state, as well as the practice of segregating HIV-positive prisoners.

Recently, there have been proposals for wider use of mandatory testing programs, sometimes referred to as "routine testing." While some have favored the mandatory testing of persons entering hospitals, the CDC has recommended that only in areas of high HIV incidence could such testing be warranted. Financially, routine blood screening is extremely costly in a low incidence area.

Routine anonymous screening of newborns has been occurring on a widespread basis for many years in a CDC-sponsored study that conceals the identity of the tested newborns. However, while such routine testing has clued epidemiologists into a picture of the pediatric transmission of HIV in the United States, it has created an ethical controversy around the issue of whether or not parents of HIV-positive children should be informed of the child's sero status. Consequently, there are now efforts to legislatively mandate that authors of newborn HIV studies make the HIV-positive status of infants known to their parents.

In turn, this issue has caused focus to shift as well to the vector for pediatric transmission of HIV—the mother. In the mid-1980s, with the discovery of its potential benefit in inhibiting the replication of HIV, AZT began a medical revolution in the way AIDS was thought of as a disease. With the discovery of other drugs used to fight HIV—a class called antiretrovirals—AIDS has been transformed from a uniformly fatal disease to one that was "treatable" simply by virtue of the fact that treatments surfaced. The advent of other antiretrovirals, coupled with increased physician knowledge on treating opportunistic infections such as pneumocystis caranii pneumonia, caused some to characterize AIDS as a disease of maintenance like diabetes or high blood pressure.

In the mid-1990s, a second revolution of thought was caused by AZT in the wake of a study that showed that AZT, when dispensed to pregnant women with HIV, lowered the potential for transmission to the newborn child by a factor of 50 percent. This medical discovery has caused many to call, therefore, for the mandatory testing of all pregnant women, so that those infected can be discovered and given AZT, thereby lessening the number of pediatric cases of AIDS in the United States.

The issue of the mandatory testing of pregnant women is fraught with emotion. It pits not only infected against uninfected but also mother against child. Early in the epidemic, there was widespread sympathy generated for babies viewed as innocent victims of the epidemic. Those who worked in the field of HIV services, and in most areas of public health, viewed anyone who contracted a virus to be an innocent victim, despite the mode of transmission. The merits of either position aside, the image of a baby as an innocent victim of a mother's HIV was and is compelling. Whether or not it is appropriate in these circumstances to pit the rights of the mother against the rights of her child, however, is doubtful. In that kind of contest, Cooper says, traditionally the mother always loses.

Liz Cooper notes that it is interesting to see the speed with which some in the scientific and medical community responded to the AZT study on newborns, compared to the intransigence of the CDC around other women and HIV issues. "It took us years and an absurd amount of energy to get the definition of AIDS expanded by the government to acknowledge the fact that HIV manifests itself differently in women than in men," she says. The fact that such manifestations were not included meant that potentially thousands of women who were ill with debilitating HIV infection were not being counted as having AIDS. In addition to not being counted, these women suffered individually when they were unable to get their social security or private disability payments. Yet, on the basis of one study, ACTG 076, which looked at AZT and newborns, many people stand poised to encourage the mandatory HIV testing of pregnant women. "Women," Cooper asserts, "are recognized as vessels, the evil people who give HIV to our children."

Women are particularly subject to legislation because of their status in society as childbearers. "It becomes easier to mandate certain behavior around women because they are or have the potential to be mothers," says Cooper.

But as is repeatedly pointed out in this book, any time the rights of one population are elevated against another in public health, then the loser is public health: "As soon as you start mandating testing, you make people think that they are criminals. If the health-care system is perceived as a criminal system, people won't come in to be tested and the harm to public health will be exponentially greater."

The mandatory testing of pregnant women has a racial impact. Considering that the overwhelming number of women infected with HIV are women of color and that, proportionally, Latinas have larger families than either Caucasian or African American women, it is easy to see that the population most affected by a repressive and compulsive measure as mandatory testing is, once again, a disenfranchised population.

The practice of mandatory testing of pregnant women undermines public health with respect not only to HIV but also to prenatal care. Keeping in mind all that is at stake when taking an HIV test, there may be women, particularly women of color who may have immigration issues to contend with, who will shun proper prenatal care out of fear of being forced to take an HIV test.

In taking the decision to test away from the mother, legislators make the tacit assumption that a properly counseled mother who is afforded the opportunity to test on her own will refuse to do so and will not act in the best interests of her baby. It is an assumption for which there is no evidence.

Finally, as pointed out earlier, reasons women often don't test for HIV include that the option is not presented to them or that if they raise the possibility, a gynecologist dismisses it. Cooper believes we should approach pregnant women differently: "Obviously by virtue of the pregnancy, the mother has engaged in a risk activity for HIV. We should give her the choice and option of testing with counseling. Over 90 percent of women consent to testing and bring themselves and their children back for care. Why don't we make healthcare professionals do their job rather than punish women for being invisible to the health-care system in the first place?"

CONCLUSION

HIV testing is a complex subject. We might prefer if it did not exist and we did not have to face up to the subject. But it is a reality of modern life in a time of an epidemic.

But there are choices about testing. They are highly personal choices, and they should be exercised with great care. The caution one must take is due to the tremendous issues of stigma and the types of discrimination one might suffer as a result of that stigma.

"If anything," says Liz Cooper, "AIDS has taught us how badly we have failed and how much work we have to do, and perhaps it will be our access point for positive change. If not, it may be used by others to create more harm. I think, though, that it really teaches us that every individual has a responsibility to get educated about HIV, to get over the stereotypes, and to interact with people the same way he interacts with every other person." We can only hope that this is less an expression of optimism than a prediction of the future.

9

No Final Victory
You and Your Doctor

*Nonetheless, he knew that the tale he had to tell
could not be one of a final victory. It could be only
the record of what had to be done and what as-
suredly would have to be done again in the never-
ending fight against terror and its relentless on-
slaughts, despite their personal afflictions, by all
who, while unable to be saints but refusing to bow
down to pestilences, strive their utmost to be healers.*

Albert Camus
The Plague

It is sometimes a difficult thing for both doctors and laypeople
to grasp the simple fact that doctors are human like anyone else.
They have the same kinds of needs, likes, dislikes, and fears. People
are often under the mistaken notion that the education physicians
receive makes them immune to prejudice, ignorance, and that most
basic of human instincts, fear.

We also expect them to be nearly godlike. We do not want to
think of them as people who get sick themselves. "Physician heal
thyself" is biblical not only in its origin but in its magnitude as well.
Society sets physicians apart in every way, sometimes on a pedestal, expecting superhuman feats of them. We do not want them to
threaten us with their illnesses, though on a daily basis we threaten
them with our own. We expect them to be all-powerful and invulnerable.

Moreover, doctors represent medical science, something that in our modern history has almost always triumphed, particularly with respect to infectious diseases. Cancer has challenged science more seriously but is not contagious or communicable like AIDS. Polio and smallpox were defeated, and tuberculosis was, for a time, pushed back. After World War II, it seemed there was little that science and medicine could not accomplish.

Then in July 1981, a small article appeared in the *New York Times*, announcing to the mainstream world the advent of a new, mysterious disease, and science teetered on its pedestal. Today, horror movies such as *Outbreak* and best-selling books such as *The Hot Zone* depict a viral scenario in which humankind is poised in innocence while mysterious illnesses wait in the shadows to attack it. With the advent of the AIDS epidemic, a real-life horror, it becomes apparent that science and medicine are not always the good that can prevail over the evil.

Physicians find themselves face to face not only with the mortality of young patients but also with their own danger. The profession has a noble history of caring for patients. During plagues and epidemics in colonial America, it was often the role of the doctor to take the patient into his own home, placing himself and his family at risk. Physicians today are still at risk, not only of contracting HIV but also for other reasons. Most risks are medical. In a survey of physicians in training at a Cook County hospital in the early 1990s, 46 percent of the physicians tested came up positive for tuberculosis. There may also be a risk from other infectious diseases, such as hepatitis, which is a significant factor for dentists.* Still, some risks are social, as in the case of the murder of physicians who perform abortions.

The realities of the AIDS epidemic, however, coupled with the fact that physicians are, in fact, only human, has meant unparal-

*In 1994, the *Washington Post* reported that in a study of 1,000 patients in a Baltimore trauma center, 25 percent of patients treated were found to have some type of infection that could be transmitted by blood. The study ran anonymous tests on patients for a 15-week period, revealing 36 people who were HIV-positive, 193 positive for hepatitis B, 146 for hepatitis C, and 16 for syphilis.

leled challenges for the medical community and for its patients. There has been a reaction to HIV in the medical community that is often, as elsewhere, based on fear. Sometimes, because of the nature of AIDS transmission, this reaction is also couched in terms of the particular moral beliefs of the physician. And, at times, the decision of a physician not to treat a person with HIV is made out of concern that it may jeopardize his or her practice; it is, therefore, merely a business decision.

In April, 1995, the *Journal of the American Dental Association* reported that a poll among dentists found that while a greater number of dentists will accept people with HIV as patients, almost a third of the dentists stated that they would never have gone into dentistry in the first place if they had known that a disease like AIDS was going to impact their practice so much.

AIDS has challenged doctors, scientists, and health-care professionals more than any other event in modern medical history, and it shakes our image of the people involved in those professions. No example of this is better known than that of Dr. David Acer, the Florida dentist who is alleged to have infected several of his patients with HIV, an event the *New York Times* dubbed "The AIDS Mystery That Won't Go Away" in July 1994. In the course of the raging epidemic there have been examples of doctors who have shown great courage, while others chose to hide behind a shield of denial, prejudice, or ignorance. As with all people, the epidemic has shown us the best and worst of what we can be. It has also shown us the vulnerable side of doctors and health-care professionals; it has shown us that they, too, can fall ill.

And when a physician does fall ill, the flames of fear in the general public have been fanned to hysteria, manifestations of which have been evident in unenlightened lawsuits. Patients sue doctors not because they contracted HIV from the doctor but because they were "afraid" that they would. In Minnesota, Dr. Phillip Benson continued to practice medicine after his diagnosis with AIDS, which, when revealed, caused great distress among his patients, who were fearful that he had been treating them while having "open lesions" on his hands. Benson was reported to have complied with universal precautions and none of his patients tested positive for HIV. In Georgia, a court ruled that a dental provider was responsible to almost 500 patients and awarded them $850,000 when one of the provider's dentists died of AIDS. This award was made based on the fear factor alone, not one of the patients having tested positive for HIV. Consequently, in Philadelphia, a court upheld the right of a hospital to require a surgeon who was HIV-positive to reveal his status to his patients. As late as 1995, a Maryland court determined that patients of an HIV-positive surgeon could sue his estate for the emotional distress they suffered when they discovered that they had been operated on by an HIV-positive surgeon. Competing levels of fear between health-care professional and patient create an environment in which final victory is not possible. However, relations between patients and their physicians do not have to be that way.

Invasive procedures on a patient known to be HIV-positive are a frightening proposition for those who must face them. Blood in an emergency procedure or in some surgeries is literally out of control. Yet the fact remains that the individual who is HIV-positive may, in fact, require surgery. And the reality is that there will be a growing body of HIV-positive people in our society. Emergency room workers, paramedics, surgeons, and dentists all face particular issues around HIV transmission and have had to reformulate the entire way they practice medicine in response to the AIDS epidemic.

This chapter will examine polls taken among physicians to determine who sees people with AIDS and who does not. It will reveal trends in thinking, some of the prejudices and facts that accompany AIDS care. What are the percent of needle sticks? This chapter meshes thematically with the rest of the book in exploring the question of the public interest versus private rights and in looking at what is at stake—access to health care.

The various challenges facing an individual with AIDS and the progress made over the past 12 years will be reviewed in a conclusion that will highlight the current state of the law as well as the challenges still facing the individual, the health-care provider, and the health-care system.

BACKGROUND

In 1988, Liz Cooper, professor at Brooklyn Law School and public interest lawyer in New York, used a computerized research system called Westlaw. She typed in the word "AIDS" to conduct a search on the cases that had involved the syndrome. She found about a dozen or so cases. Six years later, in 1994, she was again performing research. Plugging in the same term, she came up this time with over 600 cases in the federal courts alone.

The numbers of cases involving HIV continue to mount. In 1992, the American Medical Association reported that four out of five physicians in the United States had treated a person with HIV. There are not only more people with AIDS but also more laws that prohibit discriminatory actions against persons with HIV in more jurisdictions. Certainly one of the landmarks of disability legislation and of the legal history of HIV was the passage of the Americans with Disabilities Act, signed into law by George Bush in 1990 (see Chapter 5). This law prohibited discrimination against persons with a disability and, for the first time in federal legislation, included HIV/AIDS as a disability, making discrimination against persons with HIV illegal in the eyes of the federal government. AIDS laws have been passed in several states, counties, and municipal jurisdictions, and in any given year since 1985, between 300 and 500 bills regarding HIV/AIDS have appeared before the various legislatures in the United States. In short, the field of law is second only to science and medicine in the impact of AIDS. "I think that AIDS has just fundamentally changed the world and has affected the basic ways people interact with one another. The law regulates human interaction and directs it but doesn't control it," says Cooper.

It would seem clear that one of the greatest breakthroughs brought about by the Americans with Disabilities Act is the guarantee that one cannot be refused medical care because of one's disability. Yet passing a law, however clearly significant a law it may be, cannot make discrimination go away. In the first place, the law must be enforced (see Chapter 5), but, secondly, law is not absolute. Says Cooper, "When it comes to litigating over civil rights in the context of AIDS, it is really a crapshoot. We have won the basics. You can't be fired from your job if you have HIV—unless you are a health-care worker. Basically you can't be denied visitation rights if you have HIV, but there are several areas left to be litigated."

THE ADA AND ETHICAL QUESTIONS—HIV IN A MEDICAL SETTING

In 1993, a survey was published on American attitudes around the country regarding health-care professionals and HIV status. The poll, conducted by the University of California at San Francisco, revealed that 37 percent of the respondents would change doctors if they knew that their physician had tested positive and roughly the same number were concerned about the transmission of AIDS in the health-care setting. Further, of those polled, 92 percent thought that health-care workers should be tested for HIV and 93 percent believed that it should be mandatory that an infected health-care worker inform patients of his or her HIV status. In contrast, only 6 percent of patients ever asked their doctors about their doctor's HIV status.

Conversely, 89 percent also believed that health-care professionals have a right to know about the patient's status and 78 percent favored the mandatory testing of all surgery patients. Lastly, the poll revealed that among respondents who knew a person with AIDS there was less concern about issues of transmission than among those who did not know a PWA.

These views, representative of the deep-seated fear of AIDS, present a thorny dilemma for society and for the provision of medical treatment in the era of AIDS. How can there be simultaneous testing of both patient and health-care professional that is current and communicated in a way so that each party is satisfied with the other's results? How can such a thing be accomplished in a setting where the stigma of AIDS is so great, where horrendous acts of discrimination do more than violate civil rights but also cost lives and actually encourage HIV transmission? The HIV test for either patient or health-care professional raises a host of ethical dilemmas for which there is no ready, apparent answer.

The first HIV ethical dilemma occurred when the first tray was left outside the first doorway of the first patient hospitalized with AIDS back in the early 1980s in New York, San Francisco, or Los Angeles. From that point, episodes of fear, discrimination, and cruelty, both intentional and not, grew in number and magnitude. Attendants refused to clean an incontinent and helpless patient. A nurse or doctor refused to attend. An institution refused treatment. A person was tested for HIV without consent or knowledge. A doctor concealed the fact that a patient was infected from the patient himself. HIV-antibody test results were leaked, costing someone his insurance, job, family, and friends. A person stated an intention to engage in unsafe sex or needle-sharing practices. A man who was infected refused to tell a spouse who wanted to have children. A person wanted to die and asked for a doctor's help to do it. A person refused treatment. The health care professional (HCP) wanted an HIV test performed on the patient. The patient wanted an HIV test performed on the HCP. The challenges posed in HIV ethics are broad. The depth and breadth of the roots of ethical dilemmas and HIV are, respectively, very deep and complex.

Telling the Doctor You Have HIV

In February 1995, Olympic champion Greg Louganis revealed in his autobiography *Breaking the Surface* and to the media that he had a clinical diagnosis of AIDS and that he was HIV-positive and had been aware of that condition when competing in the 1988 games. This is perhaps the most famous case of the failure of a patient to reveal his HIV status to a physician. The media coverage that occurred in the wake of this announcement did not focus on the fact that an HIV-positive person won so many gold medals but rather on the potential for transmission when Louganis hit his head during a dive. He may have shed some blood in the pool. In repairing the wound, the physician neglected to wear protective gloves, despite the universal precautions set down by the Centers for Disease Control and Prevention. Why, cried columnists, didn't Louganis tell the treating doctor he had HIV? Why didn't he stop others from diving into the pool? Louganis's response was that he was frozen with fear.

Public reaction to the news of Louganis's status seemed to place the responsibility on the patient, not the physician. Little, if anything, was asked of the treating physician for his failure to employ universal precautions in treating Louganis's injury. Any failure in a physician's willingness or ability to employ universal precautions increases significantly the chance of transmission of HIV from patient to doctor. But most of the public's attention was actually on whether or not there was the possibility of transmission to other atheletes diving into the pool. Yet, despite the media focus on potential transmission in the swimming pool, there was swift and universal agreement in the medical community that the potential for such transmission was incredibly small. It was as though the media had not experienced the prior 10 years. It was asking the same elementary questions that is asked when Rock Hudson kissed Linda Evans, after learning of his status, and when Magic Johnson continued to play basketball on the court knowing his. Can you get AIDS from a kiss? Can you get AIDS from blood on the basketball court? Can you get AIDS from a swimming pool? Certainly, there was a higher risk of transmission to the treating physician. Why then did Louganis not reveal the situation to the physician?

Why indeed? The stigma of AIDS is so compelling in the medical setting that the subject is often never discussed at all. In 1993 it was reported that very few physicians or patients actually ever discuss HIV in the office, despite CDC guidelines that encourage it. In a nationwide survey, only 20 percent of the patients reported that they had ever discussed AIDS with their physician, an increase of only 5 percent since 1988. It would seem that the subject of AIDS, sex, death, and drugs are difficult to discuss in the context of the physician-patient relationship. In a separate study for the CDC, reported in 1994 from a 1992 survey of 2,545 physicians, 94 percent of them had asked a patient about smoking habits, while only 49 percent had asked about a history of sexually transmitted diseases. When it came to specifics, there was even less willingness to discuss sex, with only 31 percent inquiring about condom use, 27 percent about sexual orientation, and 22 percent about sexual partners.

When should a person with HIV tell a medical worker that they are infected with the virus? Some would say that since a medical worker should be employing universal precautions at all times, disclosure is not necessary unless there is a medical need to know about the HIV. Others would argue that it is always necessary to know HIV status, that HCPs have a right to know if someone on whom they are working under physically intimate circumstances is harboring the virus.

Both positions have flaws. If the world were perfect, there would be no need for a person with HIV to fear any consequences for disclosing his or her HIV status to an HCP. But the stigma that is attached to HIV has caused many patients to experience discrimination and humiliation at the hands of an HCP once the antibody status is revealed. In 1993, the *Chicago Tribune* reported on a study conducted by a physician at Cedars-Sinai Hospital, where 600 doctors were canvassed. It was found that there were a growing number of health-care professionals who were afraid to administer life-saving emergency procedures by giving mouth-to-mouth resuscitation. While their fear level diminished if the procedure was to be performed on a child or on someone they knew, only 15 percent of the professionals interviewed said they would do it if they knew the patient was a homosexual.

Still some feel there is a valid reason for seeking to know the status of a patient—there are over 800,000 needle sticks per year in the United States, giving a health-care worker a .3 percent chance of becoming infected with HIV in the work setting. The risk varies by profession, with needle sticks appearing to be more likely for surgical residents than for radiology residents. The fact that HIV is spreading in the population and across demographic boundaries means there is a consequential spread of risk, as evidenced by the emergence of special insurance coverage for hospitals and medical schools to cover HIV transmission in the workplace. If an HCP is facing an increased risk as a health-care worker, why should he or she not know about it? Yet, if the HCP is told that a patient is HIV-negative, then perhaps the HCP will relax attention to or dispense with universal precautions. If, in fact, the patient has had a false-negative test or is tested during the window period when the virus is present but the antibody is not, is not the HCP running a greater risk by knowing the HIV status of the patient rather than by treating each patient as a potential vector for transmission?

In California in 1991, an HIV-positive woman went to a physician's office for elective breast surgery. Frustrated by the fact that she had revealed her status to two physicians who consequently refused her treatment, she did not disclose her status to a third physician. During the procedure, when an attending nurse who was not using universal precautions accidentally cut herself with a scalpel, the fact of the patient's HIV status came to light. The nurse sued the patient. When she did so, she identified the patient. The patient countersued for a breach of confidentiality. They reached an out-of-court settlement, but the case was highly publicized and emotional, pitting the rights of the HCP against the rights of the patient. In a case like as this, there are no winners.

In Los Angeles in 1993, an HIV-positive man sought treatment for a severe cut on his hand. He first telephoned to inform the emergency care center where he was headed of his HIV status to ensure that they would treat him. When he arrived, however, the physician in charge refused to treat the hand and sent him to another facility. The man brought suit, which was settled for $85,000. The physician denied that she did anything wrong.

The Americans with Disabilities Act has been used to prohibit this kind of discrimination. Nevertheless, the real fear of a physician may result in the witholding of treatment. In Illinois, a court had to order a physician to treat a patient he had referred to another physician once the patient revealed his HIV-positive status. The patient, under treatment for a life-threatening infection, revealed his status during an interview on his medical history. The doctor suddenly refused to treat the patient and referred him elsewhere. The patient sued and the physician was ordered to treat the patient and to refrain from further violations of the ADA.

Dentistry, more than any other of medical profession, has seen reluctance to the treatment of persons who are HIV-positive. However, the Americans with Disabilities Act has been interpreted by the U.S. Justice Department to apply in the dental setting, making discrimination illegal. In what may have been the first such settlement of its kind, a Texas man received a $100,000 settlement from a dentist who had refused to treat him.

When should patients tell a health-care worker that they are HIV-positive? The answer to the question has changed over time. There was a time when it was more dangerous for a patient to reveal his or her status than it is now. The position of the ADA is clear on whether or not it is illegal to discriminate against a person with HIV. Was Greg Louganis wrong when he decided not to disclose? Was the physician wrong not to use gloves in treating him?

It is perhaps somewhat of a dodge to say that there is no right or wrong answer to these questions. As much as people may want a black or white answer, these are complex situations that require complex reasoning. To decide them one way or another as a matter of policy is to oversimplify them.

When a Health-Care Worker Has HIV

The HIV status of a health-care professional is of multiple concern. On the one hand, there is the very real danger posed to the immune compromised health-care professional exposed to several life-threatening agents. For example, a dentist is more likely to be exposed to and die of Hepatitis B Virus (HBV) than HIV in the workplace. Of even greater concern is the occupational exposure of an HIV-infected health-care worker to tuberculosis, where it has been found that an HIV-positive worker is 40 times more likely to develop TB when exposed to it than is a noninfected co-worker. On the other hand, there is an extreme fear on the part of the public of running the risk of infection from a health-care professional who has HIV disease.

Society, already terrified of AIDS, has now turned a wary eye on the HCP. Whereas calls for mandatory testing had already occurred in venues such as prisons and were proposed as prerequisites for marriage licenses and hospital admissions, after the much-publicized case of Kimberly Bergalis in Florida calls became strident for the mandatory testing of HCPs and for the mandatory retirement of an HCP found to be carrying the antibody to the virus.

The case of Bergalis and five other patients of Dr. David Acer has presented as much a mystery as tragedy, serving to target HCPs as the latest in a now long list of "risk groups." In the months following the initial discovery of the five patients, calls for the mandatory testing and retirement of health-care workers were spread across the editorial pages of the nation. In fact, so far did reaction go that some in Congress introduced legislation to make it a crime punishable by imprisonment to work in the medical fields after being infected with HIV. The fear and wariness that had once been reserved exclusively for homosexuals and drug users now followed the virus everywhere as a side effect of its transmission.

The Bergalis case is unusual but not entirely unique. Another transmission is said to have occurred in the health-care setting, though not from worker to patient. In 1994 in Australia, it was reported that a surgeon had accidentally transmitted the virus to four patients; however, the virus originated with another patient, and investigations failed to reveal precisely how the transmission from one patient to four others occurred.

The Bergalis case in particular, however, has had a strong impact on the psyche of legal policy makers as they deliberate on the issue of HIV-positive health-care workers. As with HIV-positive babies, the term "innocent victim" took on an image that is universally understood and for which all could have empathy and fear. It is transmission that can potentially occur when and where we all feel most vulnerable—in the health-care setting. Perhaps empathy fuels the sentiment. On some level, society truly believes that those who fall ill with HIV are somehow getting what they deserve because HIV is generally connected to sex, but those who receive HIV in the healthcare setting or womb are truly innocent. However, societal reaction even to "innocent victims" can be, and has been, overwhelmingly negative in particular instances, as was the case with hemophiliacs Ryan White and the Ray family, all of whom had to relocate because of the malice and fear that surrounded them in their hometowns.

Reactions, therefore, to HIV-positive HCPs are strong and usually provoke a strong response from the administration of a hospital or health department, despite the fact that there seems to be minimal risk attached to the treatment of a person by an HIV-positive HCP. Three separate studies cited in 1993 in the *San Francisco Examiner* concerned 413 patients of a Baltimore breast surgeon, 1,174 patients operated on by a surgeon over a 13-year period in New Hampshire, and 900 patients of a Miami dentist. In the first study, one patient was found to be positive but was determined to have acquired the infection from a blood transfusion. In the second study, no patients tested positive. In the third, no one showed an HIV infection that was attributable to the dentist.

Nevertheless, fear of AIDS from an HCP can reach a fever pitch. This has resulted in numerous lawsuits against a physician or institution when an HCP is known to be HIV-positive. The basis for these suits was not that there was an actual transmission of HIV from doctor to patient but that the knowledge that the physician had HIV placed the patient in such a state of fear that damage resulted and the patient was therefore due compensation.

These suits sound spurious on their face, given the statistical possibilities for contracting HIV in the health-care setting. Despite that, the suits have been plentiful and successful.

- In 1992 in Minnesota, there was a strong public reaction to a physician who died of AIDS, even though his patients all tested HIV-negative.
- In 1993 in Maryland, the state's highest court ruled that a physician could be found liable for neglecting to disclose an

HIV-positive status. The unanimous court ruling was in response to the fear expressed by two women patients who had been operated on by an HIV-positive physician. Neither woman had tested positive.

- In 1994 in Georgia, a dental association was found liable for the fact that a dentist working there failed to notify his patients of his condition. The court made an award of $850,000 to 495 patients, even though not a single patient was found to be HIV-positive.
- In late 1994, a Philadelphia hospital was found to have acted within the law when it required an HIV-positive surgeon to inform patients of his status. The physician had claimed that this was in violation of the ADA but the court did not agree, citing instead the serious circumstances around HIV exposure.

"We lack anything definitive in the case of the health-care worker, and the cases have not been going well, "says Liz Cooper. "The only thing that is sort of positive is that some of the courts have either been rejecting or limiting a recovery out of 'fear of AIDS' and we've seen a lot of fear-of-AIDS cases brought against physicians."

Cooper cites the impracticality of these lawsuits as a reason that they must ultimately fail: "To the extent that a court allows individuals to sue a physician because they found out that the physician has AIDS after the physician had operated on them, we are asking for the continuous mandatory testing of all health-care providers. That is the only way hospitals can protect themselves from lawsuits and liability. On the other hand, they would certainly face other liability from the intrusion of mandatory testing and record keeping.

"To the extent that courts limit the right of an individual to sue for fear of AIDS to those situations where there has been a breach in infection control and reason to believe that there has been exposure to bodily fluids of an individual with HIV, we are on the road to developing a sound policy and on the road to diminishing the hysteria that surrounds health-care providers."

Cooper sets a good part of the blame for these lawsuits at the feet of the CDC. "I think that a lot of the debacle of what occurred with health-care providers could have been significantly reduced had public health organizations, most particularly the CDC, stepped forward at the very beginning and said, 'HIV is not transmitted in a health-care setting, not that it can't be, but it just isn't, absent some wildly aberrational circumstances.' Recently I heard a CDC spokesperson on the radio state that when all of this happened back in 1990, we didn't really know very much about HIV in the health-care setting, and, quite frankly, I think that is bullshit.

"Some people are so eager to pin their HIV infection on behavior for which they are not responsible that I am confident that had there been other transmissions in the health-care environment, we would have known about it. And I think that the lack of leadership really has done a lot to hurt people with HIV, most particularly health-care providers with HIV, to the point where it is presumed that a health-care provider with HIV wants to hurt someone rather than help that person. And that perception is criminal."

Certainly, she argues, the disclosure of HIV is aggravated by the stigma of HIV, especially when you compare the relative risk involved of catching HIV from a health-care professional. Why, she asks, should disclosure of HIV status be required when we do not require a physician to divulge drug abuse or alcohol dependence histories? "I think that is really two questions: first—should we require these disclosures; and second—what is the relative risk with HIV compared with the harm that may occur from a physician who has a substance abuse problem? I remember when the CDC put out its first document on the relative risk in 1991. They did a whole assessment of risk and they showed that the risk of death from general anesthesia was many, many, many times greater than the risk of harm from the transmission of HIV. It is a risk that has entirely been blown out of proportion. It is not that our providers shouldn't be held to an impeccable standard but that we can't punish people for having problems, even their substance abuse, in which some sort of facilitation for care should be designed for rehabilitation."

Cooper is angry about this. "I think that if we focused on the use of universal precautions and proper infection control procedures, it is the thing that will best protect patients and best protect providers. Assumptions about an individual's HIV status will only undermine public health and individual civil liberties. This is a place where those ideals come together perfectly. And that's one thing that is really not so true about a physician's substance abuse problem. We can create a level playing field here."

Clearly, HCPs are damned if they do reveal and they are damned if they don't. Revelation of one's HIV-positive status may result in the failure of a medical practice or the transfer within a health-care institution from surgery to a field in which one is not trained or that one does not professionally desire. But failure to disclose to one's patients can result in a lawsuit that charges one with placing patients in a state of undue anxiety.

In time, it is likely that "fear" lawsuits will falter in their success. It would be extraordinary for the courts to ignore completely the evidence of the transmission rate from health-care professional to patient over a lengthy period of time. As AIDS becomes more mainstream in society, the courts may be less inclined to an emotional decision and more inclined to one based on a careful weighing of the evidence. Nevertheless, until such time, the HIV-positive HCP is in a most difficult predicament.

The Americans with Disabilties Act and Health Care

As stated in Chapter 5, the act is only as strong as those who want to enforce it. There is movement, since its passage, to water down its effectiveness by limiting its coverage to those who are visibly disabled and therefore in a wheelchair. However, in its original form, theoretically the Americans with Disabilities Act should address both the situation of the patient who is being denied health care and the health-care worker who is being denied his or her job because of HIV. Unfortunately, the wheels of justice move slowly, and such conclusions are not that obvious to the naked eye of many in the judicial system.

The act has for the most part been successful, particularly in opening access to health care for people through the defeat of insurance capping as well as preventing physicians, dentists, and health-care institutions from discriminating against persons with HIV disease. However, when it comes to protecting the health-care professional, the act has so far been a failure, and so has the legal system. In reflecting upon the changes wrought upon the legal system by AIDS, Cooper states , "In some ways, the changes have not always been good. My biggest sticking point is what happened around the health-care issue. It is very sad to me that we had very clear legal standards that simply were not applied because of AIDS phobia. It is as if AIDS phobia trumped the law. I get very angry and frustrated that this thing that is supposed to be our recourse and the great leveler has worked against us, at least in this area."

Time will tell the effectiveness of the ADA overall. The strengths and weaknesses of it as a statute will largely depend on the prevailing political climate in the executive branch of government and whether or not it will remain immune from attacks designed to water down its scope and effectiveness. To date, however, as the statute has taken hold, it appears to be on a course of success, at least in terms of making access to health care a right in the eyes of the law. "I'd certainly rather have it than not have it," says Cooper. "You can't legislate the end of discrimination. You can't change what people have in their hearts merely by passing a law. At the same time, we'll have no chance of challenging stereotypes and changing public perceptions with the absence of laws like the ADA."

CONCLUSION

As was pointed out in the beginning of this book, when the epidemic emerged everyone wanted to pretend that AIDS was someone else's problem, that it belonged to an "other" kind of person out there in society: "As long as I am good and do nothing wrong, it will not come into my house." But clearly, as this chapter shows, AIDS does come into people's homes uninvited. AIDS was not brought here by anyone's behavior. It is just here. If nothing else, this chapter demonstrates the theme of this book dramatically:

the problems and challenges of AIDS and HIV that are faced by a single person have to be faced by every person. What we would like to think is one person's problem is, in fact, everyone's problem. The same dilemma faced by a person with AIDS in deciding to tell his physician about his HIV status is faced by all physicians vis-à-vis their patients. AIDS is in one place and everywhere, all at the same time.

The ethics of the disclosure situation are not easily solved by the legal system. The legal system cannot instill values in people; rather it is a reflection of the values of society. It is difficult, then, to state that there is a clear right or wrong answer to the situations presented here. Rather, there must, in each situation, be a solid application of reason, a policy process that leaves out the emotional factor, to determine what will be in the best interests of the individuals involved and what will be in the best interests of society. In each circumstance, any answer that pits one against another will be the wrong choice. In AIDS public health, there are clearly ways to solve such dilemmas without sacrificing the interests of the infected over the uninfected. What is also clear is that traveling down the road of sound reason requires a great deal of work and commitment.

Conclusion

Law bestows no rights on you. Your rights belong to you inherently. Law merely issues you the tools with which to meet the challenges you encounter in society. Some of the tools you can use early, to prevent disaster; others can be used after disaster has occurred. But if there is one theme that stands out from these pages it is that of planning. The legal pitfalls for a person with AIDS or for an institution that encounters people with AIDS can, for the most part, be anticipated and avoided, given careful planning. This sounds simple but in reality it is a lot to ask.

When people discover that their immune system is compromised because a foreign agent has entered their bloodstream, it is not unlike the experience of being diagnosed with any other life-threatening illness. There is a feeling of betrayal as one realizes that one's own body is letting one down. The fact that the foreign agent, HIV, has been so successful in killing its hosts, combined with the fact that there is so much judgment and stigma heaped upon those who have it, adds even more burden. The belief, among many, that one has this disease in the first place because of acts of sex engaged in and because of who one is brings a pressure to bear that is unlike any other disease in history. The fact that there is no cure is an almost insurmountable obstacle.

The consequence of all of this is often that a person feels a complete loss of control over what is going on inside and outside of his or her body. People, even those with the best of intentions, begin to treat you differently. The fact is that you are different now than you were before your diagnosis, but the way people treat you may not be the way you want to be treated. They may treat you like a person who is dying. They may treat you like a victim. They may try to make you into a victim. The fact is, though, that through good medical intervention and attention to your physical well-being, people with HIV can lengthen their lives and give themselves time to improve the quality of their lives dramatically. It is also possible to be overcome with despair or a feeling that you can never again control what is going to happen to you.

It takes a strong person to recover from the diagnosis of HIV infection. Yet recovery is key. And just as recovery requires a careful attention to medical interventions and the administration to you of prophylaxes for opportunistic infections, so must you be prepared to be proactive with respect to the legal aspects of your situation. To do otherwise invites more victimization.

As David Schulman stated in Chapter 5, every person, after seeing a competent physician, ought to go for a good legal checkup. You can go through what you might perceive as a morbid experience by writing a will, yet in the end feel that you have gone out and gotten some rights that had always been denied you. You can arrange to have others make medical decisions for you if you cannot make your own. You can ensure the safety of your children and soften the reality of the situation they are facing with you. To protect your finances, which have the potential to be spiraling out of control, there are steps you can take to ensure your security, both in terms of debt management and negotiating the labyrinth of difficulties surrounding entitlement and disability programs. Discrimination, a manifestation of society's fear of HIV, is not something you need to suffer in housing, employment, or public accommodation. You can do damage control by knowing how and when to tell an employer about your situation. Your access to quality health care may be dependent on whether or not you have insurance or can maintain it if you do have it. Even when and where you test for HIV and the manner of the dissemination of your test results may complicate your situation by compromising your access to healthcare; it can be further put at risk if your health-care provider is not one who is willing to treat people with HIV. These are the most common challenges facing people with HIV and yet in facing these issues early and preparing and planning for the possible roadblocks you may face, you may find that the process of doing such planning heightens an awareness in you of what control you do have over your situation, heading off anyone who would turn you into an AIDS "victim."

Similarly, the sense that we are "in control" of the epidemic is necessary in order for society to feel secure. Policy makers are often guided by the wish to establish that control, or at the very least, to give the appearance that we are controlling the epidemic by controlling the people who are infected.

The state of the law with respect to AIDS is and will continue to be in a state of flux. This is not a failure in the law but rather a reflection of the complexity and the changing nature of the epidemic itself.

It is important not to expect too much of the law. Law is nothing more than the embodiment in code and practice of the values and ethics we hold as a society. Law is a mirror image of those values, and sometimes those values let us down. That does not mean that the system does not work; it means that we are unclear, as a society, about our priorities. Oftentimes, society has not worked out its own conflicts. The law is not the end to achieving rights and overcoming challenges; it is the means. It is the tool that you will use to bring about your own solutions.

Laws change to reflect society's values. Political winds shift and the law, as an expression of political will, must also bend frequently. At times, it will work more closely in conjunction with the interests of people with AIDS than at other times. For that reason, knowledge of, understanding of, and activism in the politics of AIDS is all-important, because it is in the political arena that the tools given you by the law will be either enhanced or diminished. It is there that it will be determined whether you are a person living with AIDS or an AIDS victim.

Appendixes

A. Medical Power of Attorney

California Medical Association
Durable Power of Attorney for Health Care
Decisions
(California Probate Code Sections 4600-4753)*

WARNING TO PERSONS EXECUTING THIS DOCUMENT

This is an important legal document. Before executing this document, you should know these important facts:

This document gives the person you designate as your agent (the attorney-in-fact) the power to make health-care decisions for you. Your agent must act consistently with your desires as stated in this document or otherwise made known.

Except as you otherwise specify in this document, this document gives your agent power to consent to your doctor's not giving treatment or stopping treatment that would be necessary to keep you alive.

Notwithstanding this document, you have the right to make medical and other health-care decisions for yourself so long as you can give informed consent with respect to the particular decision. In addition, no treatment may be given to you over your objection, and health-care necessary to keep you alive may not be stopped or withheld if you object at the time.

*Copyright California Medical Association 1995. Published with permission of and by arrangement with the California Medical Association. Copies of this form, as well as an accompanying brochure and wallet card, may be obtained from CMA Publications at 800-882-1-CMA.

This document gives your agent authority to consent, to refuse to consent, or to withdraw consent to any care, treatment, service, or procedure to maintain, diagnose, or treat a physical or mental condition. This power is subject to any statement of your desires and any limitations that you include in this document. You may state in this document any types of treatment that you do not desire. In addition, a court can take away the power of your agent to make health-care decisions for you if your agent (1) authorizes anything that is illegal, (2) acts contrary to your known desires, or (3) where your desires are not known, does anything that is clearly contrary to your best interests.

This power will exist for an indefinite period of time unless you limit its duration in this document.

You have the right to revoke the authority of your agent by notifying your agent or your treating doctor, hospital, or other health-care provider orally or in writing of the revocation.

Your agent has the right to examine your medical records and to consent to their disclosure unless you limit this right in this document. Unless you specify otherwise in this document, this document gives your agent the power after you die to (1) authorize an autopsy, (2) donate your body or parts thereof for transplant, therapeutic, educational, scientific purposes, and (3) direct the disposition of your remains.

If there is anything in this document that you do not understand, you should ask a lawyer to explain it to you.

1. Creation of Durable Power of Attorney for Health Care

By this document I intend to create a durable power of attorney by appointing the person designated below to make health-care decisions for me as allowed by Sections 4600 to 4753 inclusive of the California Penal Code. This power of attorney shall not be affected by my subsequent incapacity. I hereby revoke any prior durable power of attorney for health care. I am a California resident who is at least 18 years old, of sound mind, and acting of my own free will.

2. Appointment of Health Care Agent

Fill in below the name, address, and telephone number of the person you wish to make health-care decisions for you if you become incapacitated. You should make sure that this person agrees to accept this responsibility. The following may not serve as your agent: (1) your treating health-care provider; (2) an operator of a community care facility or residential care facility for the elderly; or (3) an employee of your treating health-care provider, a community care facility, or a residential care facility for the elderly, unless that employee is related to you by blood, marriage, or adoption. If you are a conservatee under the Lanterman-Petris-Short Act (the law governing involuntary commitment to a mental health facility) and you wish to appoint your conservator as your agent, you must consult a lawyer, who must sign and attach a special declaration for this document to be valid.

I, _____ , hereby appoint:

Name _____

Address _____

Work Telephone (___)_____ Home Telephone (___) _____

as my agent (attorney-in-fact) to make health-care decisions for me as authorized in this document. I understand that this power of attorney will be effective for an indefinite period of time unless I revoke it or limit its duration below.

Optional: This power of attorney shall expire on the following date:

_____

3. Authority of Agent

If I become incapable of giving informed consent for health-care decisions, I grant my agent full power and authority to make those decisions for me, subject to any statements of desires or limitations set forth below. Unless I have limited my agent's authority in this document, that authority shall include the right to consent, refuse consent, or withdraw consent to any medical care, treatment, service, or procedure; to receive and to consent to the release of medical information; to authorize an autopsy to determine the cause of my death; to make a gift of all or part of my body; and to direct the disposition of my remains, subject to any instructions I have given in a written contract for funeral services, my will, or some other method. I understand that, by law, my agent may *not* consent to any of the following: commitment to a mental health treatment facility, convulsive treatment, psychosurgery, sterilization, or abortion.

4. Medical Treatment Desires and Limitations (optional)

Your agent must make health-care decisions that are consistent with your known desires. You may, but are not required to, state your desires about the kinds of medical care you do or do not want to receive, including your desires concerning life support if you are seriously ill. If you do not want your agent to have the authority to make certain decisions, you must write a statement to that effect in the space provided below; otherwise, your agent will have the broad powers to make health-care decisions for you that are outlined in paragraph 3 above. In either case, it is important that you discuss your health-care desires with the person you appoint as your agent, and with your doctors.

Following is a general statement about withholding and removal of life-sustaining treatment. If the statement accurately reflects your desires, you may initial it. If you wish to add to it or to write your own statement instead, you may do so in the space provied.

I do not want efforts made to prolong my life and I do not want life-sustaining treatment to be provided or continued: (1) if I am in an irreversible coma or persistent vegetative state; or (2) if I am terminally ill and the use of life-sustaining procedures would serve only to artificially delay the moment of my death; or (3) under any other circumstances where the burdens of the treatment outweigh the expected benefits. In making decisions about life-sustaining treatment under provision (3) above, I want my agent to consider the relief of suffering and the quality of my life, as well as the extent of the possible prolongation of my life.

If this statement reflects your desires, initial here: _____

Other or additional statements of medical treatment desires and limitations:

_____

_____

_____

_____

You may attach additional pages if you need more space to complete your statements. Each additional page must be dated and signed at the same time you date and sign this document.

5. Appointment of Alternate Agents (optional)

You may appoint alternate agents to make health-care decisions for you in case the person you appointed in Paragraph 2 is unable or unwilling to do so.

If the person named as my agent in Paragraph 2 is not available or willing to make health-care decisions for me as authorized in this document, I appoint the following persons to do so, listed in the order they should be asked:

First Alternate Agent:

Name _____ Work Telephone (___) _____

Address_____ Home Telephone (___) _____

Second Alternate Agent:

Name: _____ Work Telephone (___) _____

Address _____ Home Telephone (___) _____

6. Use of Copies

I hereby authorize that photocopies of this document can be relied upon by my agent and others as though they were originals.

I sign my name to this Durable Power of Attorney for Health Care at [CITY] _____ , [STATE] ____ , on [DATE] _____ ,

SIGNATURE OF PRINCIPAL _____

STATEMENT OF WITNESSES

This power of attorney will not be valid for making health-care decisions unless it is either (1) signed by two qualified adult witnesses who know you personally (or to whom you present evidence of your identity) and who are present when you sign or acknowledge your signature or (2) acknowledged before a notary public in California. If you elect to use witnesses rather than a notary public, the law provides that none of the following may be used as witnesses: (1) the persons you have appointed as your agent and alternate agents; (2) your health-care provider or an employee of your health-care provider; or (3) an operator or employee of an operator of a community care facility or residential care facility for the elderly. Additionally, at least one of the witnesses cannot be related to you by blood, marriage, or adoption, or be named in your will. IF YOU ARE A PATIENT IN A SKILLED NURSING FACILITY, YOU MUST HAVE A PATIENT ADVOCATE OR OMBUDSMAN SIGN BOTH THE STATEMENT OF WITNESSES BELOW AND THE DECLARATION ON THE FOLLOWING PAGE.

I declare under penalty of perjury under the laws of California that the person who signed or acknowledged this document is personally known to me to be the principal, or that the identity of the principal was proved to me by convincing evidence* that the principal signed or acknowledged this durable power of attorney in my presence, that the principal appears to be of sound mind and under no duress, fraud, or undue influence; that I am not the person appointed as attorney-in-fact by this document; and that I am not the principal's health-care provider, an employee of the principal's health-care provider, the operator of a community care facility or residential care facility for the elderly, or an employee of an operator of a community care facility or residential care facility for the elderly.

(At least one of the above witnesses must also sign the following declaration)

Signature _____   Signature _____

Print Name _____   Print Name _____

Date _____   Date _____

Residence Address _____   Residence Address _____

_____   _____

I further declare under penalty of perjury under the laws of California that I am not related to the principal by blood, marriage, or adoption, and, to the best of my knowledge I am not entitled to any part of the estate of the principal upon the death of the principal under a will now existing or by operation of law.

Signature _____

*The law allows one or more of the following forms of identification as convincing evidence of identity: a California driver's license or identification card or U.S. passport that is current or has been issued within five years, contains a photograph and description of the person named on it, is signed by that person, and bears a serial or other identifying number; a foreign passport that has been stamped by the U.S. Immigration and Naturalization Service; a driver's license issued by another state or by an authorized Canadian or Mexican agency; or an identification card issued by another state or by any branch of the U.S. armed forces. If the principal is a patient in a skilled nursing facility, a patient advocate or ombudsman may rely on the representations of family members or the administrator or staff of the facility as convincing evidence of identity if the patient advocate or ombudsman believes that the representations provide a reasonable basis for determining the identity of the principal.

Special Requirement: Statement of Patient Advocate or Ombudsman (If you are a patient in a skilled nursing facility, a patient advocate or ombudsman must sign the

Statement of Witness above and must also sign the following declaration.)

I further declare under penalty of perjury under the laws of California that I am a patient advocate or ombudsman as designated by the State Department of Aging and am serving as a witness as required by subdivision (e) of Probate Code Section 4701.

Signature: _____ Address: _____
Print Name: _____   _____
Date: _____   _____

Certificate of Acknowledgement of Notary Public

Acknowledgement before a notary public is not required if you have elected to have two qualified witnesses sign above. If you are a patient in a skilled nursing facility you must have a patient advocate or ombudsman sign the Statement of Witnesses on page 3 and the Statement of Patient Advocate or Ombudsman above.

State of California   )
County of   _____)

On this _____ day of _____, in the year _____, before me, _____ (name of notary) _____ personally appeared (_____insert name of principal _____), personally known to me (or proved to me on the basis of satisfactory evidence) to be the person(s) whose name(s) is/are subscribed to this instrument and acknowledged to me that he/she/they executed the same in his/her/their authorized capacity(ies), and that by his/her/their signature(s) on the instrument the person(s), or the entity upon behalf of which the person(s) acted, executed the instrument.

WITNESS my hand and official seal.

_____
Signature of Notary Public   NOTARY SEAL

B. Appointment of Guardian

New York State

I, [NAME] _____ , hereby designate [NAME OF PROPOSED GUARDIAN] _____ residing at [ADDRESS AND TELEPHONE NUMBER OF PROPOSED GUARDIAN] _____ , as standby guardian of [NAME(S) OF MINOR CHILD(REN)]_____ .

The standby guardian's authority shall take effect if and when either (1) my doctor concludes that I am mentally incapacitated and thus unable to care for my child(ren); or (2) my doctor concludes that I am physically debilitated and thus unable to care for my child(ren), and I consent in writing, before two witnesses, to the standby guardian's authority taking effect.

In the event the person I designate is unable or unwilling to act as guardian for my child(ren), I hereby designate [NAME, HOME ADDRESS, AND TELEPHONE NUMBER OF ALTERNATE GUARDIAN]_____ , as standby guardian of my child(ren).

I also understand that my standby guardian's authority will cease 60 days after it commences unless by such date he or she petitions the court for appointment as guardian.

I understand that I retain parental rights even after the commencement of the standby guardian's authority and may revoke the standby guardianship at any time.

Signature _____

Address _____

Date _____

I declare that the person whose name appears above signed this document in my presence, or was physically unable to sign and asked another to sign this document, who did so in my presence. I further declare that I am at least 18 years old and am not the person designated as the standby guardian.

Witness's _____

Address _____

_____

Date _____

Witness's _____

Address _____

_____

Date _____

C. State-by-State Breakdown of Living Wills and Health Care Agent Laws*

The following 45 states† allow *both* a living will *and* the appointment of a health-care agent:

Arizona	Louisiana	Oklahoma
Arkansas	Maine	Oregon
California	Maryland	Pennsylvania
Colorado	Minnesota	Rhode Island
Connecticut	Mississippi	South Carolina
Delaware	Missouri	South Dakota
Florida	Montana	Tennessee
Georgia	Nebraska	Texas
Hawaii	Nevada	Utah
Idaho	New Hampshire	Vermont
Illinois	New Jersey	Virginia
Indiana	New Mexico	Washington
Iowa	North Carolina	West Virginia
Kansas	North Dakota	Wisconsin
Kentucky	Ohio	Wyoming

States that authorize *only* living wills are the following:

Alabama
Alaska

States that authorize *only* the appointment of a healthcare agent are the following:

Massachusetts
Michigan
New York

*Information supplied by Choice in Dying, New York, NY.
†In addition, the District of Columbia also falls within this category.

D. State Positions on Forced Feeding and Hydration*

The following 34 states *permit* refusal of a person to accept artificial nutrition and hydration through his or her living will:

Alaska	Louisiana	Oregon
Arizona†	Maine	Pennsylvania
California	Maryland	Rhode Island
Colorado	Minnesota	South Carolina
Connecticut	Nevada	South Dakota
Georgia	New Jersey	Tennessee
Hawaii	New Hampshire	Utah
Idaho	North Carolina	Virginia
Illinois‡	North Dakota	Washington
Indiana	Ohio	Wisconsin
Iowa	Oklahoma	Wyoming
Kentucky		

States with living will statutes that *do not permit* the withdrawal of food and hydration:

Missouri—except that a duly appointed agent may choose to forgo such treatment

*Not specifically mentioned in the statute text.
†Cannot be withheld if death will be due to starvation or hydration.
‡Information supplied by Choice in Dying, New York, NY.

States that do not have statutes that specifically address this issue:

District of Columbia	Montana
Alabama	Nebraska
Arkansas	New Mexico
Delaware	Texas
Florida	Vermont
Kansas	West Virginia

States that do not have living will statutes:

Massachusetts
Michigan
New York

E. States that Require HIV Names Reporting

Alabama	Minnesota	South Carolina
Arizona	Mississippi	South Dakoka
Arkansas	Missouri	Tennessee
Colorado	Nevada	Utah
Connecticut	New Jersey	Virginia
Idaho	North Carolina	West Virginia
Indiana	North Dakota	Wisconsin
Louisiana	Ohio	Wyoming
Michigan	Oklahoma	

Glossary of Terms

Accelerated Life Insurance Benefit—The prepayment to the insured of a portion of the amount that would become due upon death and that would be payable to the designated beneficiary of the policy. It is different from a viatical settlement in that the policy is cashed in early with the insurance company, not sold to a third party.

Administrator of an Estate—This person has a role very similar to the executor of an estate, who is appointed when there is a will. If a person dies without a will, an administrator will be appointed to oversee the estate and see to its responsibilities, paying all debts and expenses and then disbursing to those who inherit as a result of being the next of kin to the deceased.

Alternate Beneficiary—A person named in a will or in the beneficiary statement accompanying a testamentary who receives the property only if another individual, first designated in the document, fails to survive the owner of the property.

Americans with Disabilities Act—Passed by Congress and signed into law in 1990, this law makes it illegal to discriminate against persons with a disability in public accommodation or places of employment. The act is enforced by the United States Justice Department.

Anonymous Testing—HIV-antibody testing that is done without providing one's name.

Bequest—A gift made in a last will and testament.

Beneficiary—A person named in a last will and testament who will receive a gift under the terms of the will.

Capping—The practice by insurance companies or by employers of limiting the amount of money that will be spent under the terms of a policy of health insurance to a specific amount for a specific disease condition.

COBRA—The Consolidated Omnibus Reconciliation Act passed in 1985, allowing people who leave employment for any reason, except their own gross misconduct, to retain for a set period of time their group insurance plan, as long as they pay for their share of the group's premiums.

Confidential Testing—HIV-antibody testing in which one's name is taken and kept confidential.

Contact Tracing—The process by which a health department notifies the sexual or needle-sharing contact of a person diagnosed with HIV that there is a risk of exposure and promotes the consequent testing of that third party.

Contingency Fee—An agreement made with an attorney or law firm that one's case will be taken on without an up-front payment from the client but will be paid from the proceeds of any reward, judgment, or settlement that occurs as a result. Most often used in tort situations. Sometimes in spite of this arrangement expenses of the lawsuit still have to be paid by the client.

Disability Insurance—A policy of insurance that, upon proof of disability, pays to the recipient a portion of his or her former salary for the duration of the disability.

Durable Power of Attorney—A power of attorney the validity of which is unaffected by a subsequent disability of the person who signed it (see also Power of Attorney).

Employee Retirement Income Security Act (ERISA)—Federal law that, among other things, regulates the activities of employers who are self-insured.

Executor—A person named in a last will and testament to discharge the will and see to it that everything is done in accordance with law and the terms of the will.

Health Maintenance Organizations (HMOs)—A plan of health coverage designed to bring together people under a closed operation of health provision, meaning that only people enrolled in the organization use its facilities and that those people may only use the organization's health facilities. In essence, it is similar to belonging to a health club, only it is a health-care club. It is unique in its ability to provide coverage without imposing a preexisting condition term.

High-Risk Pools—Health insurance groups formed by states usually in conjunction with private insurers to provide insurance policies to people who are otherwise "uninsurable" because of a preexisting condition at a cost usually between 150 and 300 percent greater than regular insurance.

Indemnity Plan—A health insurance plan that is very traditional, it allows a covered person to see any physician of his or her choice and pays a certain percentage of the costs associated with the health provision. It is generally the most expensive type of coverage available.

In Terrorem Clause—This clause contained in a last will and testament that states that if any person who is named in the will as a beneficiary challenges the validity of the will and then loses the will contest, he or she forfeits the bequest made to him or her under the terms of the will.

Intestate—The state of being without a valid will, thereby having property distributed to one's legatees by operation of law after one's death.

Last Will and Testament—A document by which you delegate your rights in tangible and intangible property, to take effect after your death.

Legatee—From the word "legacy," a person who would inherit property automatically by virtue of being the next in the natural line of inheritance by operation of law and whose interests are often affected, if not eliminated, by the making of a last will and testament.

Living Will—A written instrument, which may have a different name in various states, that enunciates your desires with respect to medical treatment. It is most often used to state that extraordinary means to keep you alive should or should not be used, and in what manner.

Mandatory Names Reporting—The practice, imposed by a state, to require that the names and addresses of all those people in the state who test positive for the HIV antibody be reported to the health department.

Material Misrepresentation—An omission of something from your medical background, or an out-and-out fabrication regarding your medical condition, which would have affected the insurance company's decision to issue the policy to you.

Medicaid—A form of government health insurance for the poor, covering prescriptions and hospitalizations. This program has income and asset restrictions and severely restricts one's ability to access health care.

Medical Power of Attorney—Sometimes called a directive to a physician, or other, similar terms, this is a document by which one bestows the authority to make medical decisions on a third party if one cannot make one's own medical decisions.

Medicare—A form of government health insurance for the disabled and elderly with eligibility determined by length of disability and not income, this program is more generous than Medicaid, and access to health care is higher.

Power of Attorney—This document allows you to delegate your rights to another individual to do that which you normally would do yourself, for use during your lifetime, for whatever period of time and for whatever reason you may deem proper.

Preexisting Condition—A medical condition that you had, or should have reasonably known that you had, at the time you became covered by a health insurance policy.

Preexisting Condition Term—The period of time written into your health insurance policy, during which the policy will not pay for a condition that you had, or should have reasonably known that you had, at the time you became covered by it.

Preferred Provider Organizations (PPOs)—A health plan that combines the characteristics of both HMOs and indemnity plans by having a set of health-care providers for whom coverage is automatic, but allowing a person to see health-care providers outside the established network with a lower rate of coverage.

Presumptive Disability—The issuance of supplemental disability payments (SSI) from the Social Security Administration based on the fact that you have a diagnosis of AIDS. You are therefore eligible to receive social security payments while your claim is being processed.

Probate—The process by which a court reviews a last will and testament to determine its validity; it is only after this process that the will can actually take effect.

Rescission of Policy—Applied to life, health, and disability insurance, this is the act of treating a policy for insurance, as if it never existed at all. Involving the return of all premiums paid to the consumer, this occurs within a window period of contestability.

Redlining—The practice by insurance companies of segmenting certain geographical areas or professions, charging higher rates or denying insurance altogether because of an association of risk connected to people based on who they are or where they live rather than on their individual backgrounds.

Residuary Estate—That part of a testamentary estate that is left after the payment of debts and expenses and after specific bequests to beneficiaries are made.

Routine Testing—Often a term used to mask a program of mandatory testing, that is HIV testing that is not anonymous but that everyone participating in a particular service or event must take. For example, there was discussion of the routine testing of hospital patients or the routine testing of NBA basketball players after the diagnosis of Magic Johnson with HIV.

Secured Transaction—When you guarantee that you will pay back money you borrow by giving the lender an interest in a physical asset called collateral.

Self-Insured Companies—An employer who, rather than purchase insurance, insures its employees through the formation of its own plan, which is regulated by ERISA and tempered by the Americans with Disabilities Act.

Social Security Disability Insurance (SSDI)—A government-sponsored disability insurance program that will pay you a set amount on a monthly basis during the period of your disability. Eligibility for this program is contingent on whether you have worked for an employer who paid into the system for you, as indicated by the FICA designation on your pay stub.

Springing Power of Attorney—This power of attorney instrument only becomes effective upon the occurrence of an event, such as disability (see also Power of Attorney).

Standby Guardianship—Making provision to designate the guardians of your children so that in the event of your death it is clear with whom the children will be placed. In some states, this may be a form of temporary guardianship.

State Supplementary Payments (SSPs)—Payments that may be made under programs that exist within your state and that will be taken into account when determining whether you will receive any supplemental security income from the federal government.

Supplemental Security Income (SSI)—A supplemental amount of income paid by the government to people who are disabled and who have incomes that are under a set ceiling. The amount may vary from state to state. To qualify, people must have very little in assets (not including home and automobile).

Temporary Guardianship—A legal provision for the temporary placement of a child, usually during the parent's illness or brief incapacitation.

Testamentary Estate—That part of one's property which is given away under the terms of a last will and testament.

Testamentary Substitute—That part of one's property which is not given away under the terms of a last will and testament but rather passes to another individual by operation of law upon one's death. An example is a life insurance policy naming a specific beneficiary; this is a testamentary substitute and is not affected by a last will and testament.

Testate—The state of having a valid will.

Undue Influence—In the context of writing a will, this is when a person exerts influence upon another person to make bequests that the testator otherwise would not have made because he is being influenced by a power of persuasion that causes him to act in a way he otherwise would not have done.

Unsecured Transaction—This is when you borrow money but there is no collateral put up for the loan, only a promise to pay.

Viatical Settlement—From the Latin *viaticus,* meaning the blessing given to the dying, this refers to a settlement with an company that, in effect, buys from you the interest in the payment from your life insurance policy for a sum that is an agreed-upon fraction of the policy value. It differs from accelerated payment in that you are in effect "selling" your life insurance to a third party as opposed to cashing it in early.

INDEX

Mark S. Senak, J.D., was newly graduated from Brooklyn Law School in the early days of the AIDS epidemic. He began volunteering legal services for people with AIDS (PWAs) in 1983 with the Bar Association for Human Rights of Greater New York and then began working full-time in 1985 at Gay Men's Health Crisis. When he left this position (and New York) three years later, the *New York Times* credited Mr. Senak's office with having delivered legal services to 10 percent of all existing cases of PWAs in this country. A frequent lecturer and author on various aspects of HIV, AIDS, law, and ethics, the author is currently Director of Planning at AIDS Project Los Angeles and sits on the Public Policy Committee of the AIDS Action Council in Washington, D.C. He resides in Hollywood, California.